T&P BOOKS

I0170855

KYRGYZ
VOCABULARY

FOR ENGLISH SPEAKERS

ENGLISH-
KYRGYZ

The most useful words
To expand your lexicon and sharpen
your language skills

3000 words

Kyrgyz vocabulary for English speakers - 3000 words

By Andrey Taranov

T&P Books vocabularies are intended for helping you learn, memorize and review foreign words. The dictionary is divided into themes, covering all major spheres of everyday activities, business, science, culture, etc.

The process of learning words using T&P Books' theme-based dictionaries gives you the following advantages:

- Correctly grouped source information predetermines success at subsequent stages of word memorization
- Availability of words derived from the same root allowing memorization of word units (rather than separate words)
- Small units of words facilitate the process of establishing associative links needed for consolidation of vocabulary
- Level of language knowledge can be estimated by the number of learned words

T&P Books Publishing
www.tpbooks.com

ISBN: 978-1-78767-014-3

This book is also available in E-book formats.
Please visit www.tpbooks.com or the major online bookstores.

KYRGYZ VOCABULARY
for English speakers

T&P Books vocabularies are intended to help you learn, memorize, and review foreign words. The vocabulary contains over 3000 commonly used words arranged thematically.

- Vocabulary contains the most commonly used words
- Recommended as an addition to any language course
- Meets the needs of beginners and advanced learners of foreign languages
- Convenient for daily use, revision sessions, and self-testing activities
- Allows you to assess your vocabulary

Special features of the vocabulary

- Words are organized according to their meaning, not alphabetically
- Words are presented in three columns to facilitate the reviewing and self-testing processes
- Words in groups are divided into small blocks to facilitate the learning process
- The vocabulary offers a convenient and simple transcription of each foreign word

The vocabulary has 101 topics including:

Basic Concepts, Numbers, Colors, Months, Seasons, Units of Measurement, Clothing & Accessories, Food & Nutrition, Restaurant, Family Members, Relatives, Character, Feelings, Emotions, Diseases, City, Town, Sightseeing, Shopping, Money, House, Home, Office, Working in the Office, Import & Export, Marketing, Job Search, Sports, Education, Computer, Internet, Tools, Nature, Countries, Nationalities and more ...

T&P BOOKS' THEME-BASED DICTIONARIES

The Correct System for Memorizing Foreign Words

Acquiring vocabulary is one of the most important elements of learning a foreign language, because words allow us to express our thoughts, ask questions, and provide answers. An inadequate vocabulary can impede communication with a foreigner and make it difficult to understand a book or movie well.

The pace of activity in all spheres of modern life, including the learning of modern languages, has increased. Today, we need to memorize large amounts of information (grammar rules, foreign words, etc.) within a short period. However, this does not need to be difficult. All you need to do is to choose the right training materials, learn a few special techniques, and develop your individual training system.

Having a system is critical to the process of language learning. Many people fail to succeed in this regard; they cannot master a foreign language because they fail to follow a system comprised of selecting materials, organizing lessons, arranging new words to be learned, and so on. The lack of a system causes confusion and eventually, lowers self-confidence.

T&P Books' theme-based dictionaries can be included in the list of elements needed for creating an effective system for learning foreign words. These dictionaries were specially developed for learning purposes and are meant to help students effectively memorize words and expand their vocabulary.

Generally speaking, the process of learning words consists of three main elements:

- Reception (creation or acquisition) of a training material, such as a word list
- Work aimed at memorizing new words
- Work aimed at reviewing the learned words, such as self-testing

All three elements are equally important since they determine the quality of work and the final result. All three processes require certain skills and a well-thought-out approach.

New words are often encountered quite randomly when learning a foreign language and it may be difficult to include them all in a unified list. As a result, these words remain written on scraps of paper, in book margins, textbooks, and so on. In order to systematize such words, we have to create and continually update a "book of new words." A paper notebook, a netbook, or a tablet PC can be used for these purposes.

This "book of new words" will be your personal, unique list of words. However, it will only contain the words that you came across during the learning process. For example, you might have written down the words "Sunday," "Tuesday," and "Friday." However, there are additional words for days of the week, for example, "Saturday," that are missing, and your list of words would be incomplete. Using a theme dictionary, in addition to the "book of new words," is a reasonable solution to this problem.

The theme-based dictionary may serve as the basis for expanding your vocabulary.

It will be your big "book of new words" containing the most frequently used words of a foreign language already included. There are quite a few theme-based dictionaries available, and you should ensure that you make the right choice in order to get the maximum benefit from your purchase.

Therefore, we suggest using theme-based dictionaries from T&P Books Publishing as an aid to learning foreign words. Our books are specially developed for effective use in the sphere of vocabulary systematization, expansion and review.

Theme-based dictionaries are not a magical solution to learning new words. However, they can serve as your main database to aid foreign-language acquisition. Apart from theme dictionaries, you can have copybooks for writing down new words, flash cards, glossaries for various texts, as well as other resources; however, a good theme dictionary will always remain your primary collection of words.

T&P Books' theme-based dictionaries are specialty books that contain the most frequently used words in a language.

The main characteristic of such dictionaries is the division of words into themes. For example, the *City* theme contains the words "street," "crossroads," "square," "fountain," and so on. The *Talking* theme might contain words like "to talk," "to ask," "question," and "answer".

All the words in a theme are divided into smaller units, each comprising 3–5 words. Such an arrangement improves the perception of words and makes the learning process less tiresome. Each unit contains a selection of words with similar meanings or identical roots. This allows you to learn words in small groups and establish other associative links that have a positive effect on memorization.

The words on each page are placed in three columns: a word in your native language, its translation, and its transcription. Such positioning allows for the use of techniques for effective memorization. After closing the translation column, you can flip through and review foreign words, and vice versa. "This is an easy and convenient method of review – one that we recommend you do often."

Our theme-based dictionaries contain transcriptions for all the foreign words. Unfortunately, none of the existing transcriptions are able to convey the exact nuances of foreign pronunciation. That is why we recommend using the transcriptions only as a supplementary learning aid. Correct pronunciation can only be acquired with the help of sound. Therefore our collection includes audio theme-based dictionaries.

The process of learning words using T&P Books' theme-based dictionaries gives you the following advantages:

- You have correctly grouped source information, which predetermines your success at subsequent stages of word memorization
- Availability of words derived from the same root (lazy, lazily, lazybones), allowing you to memorize word units instead of separate words
- Small units of words facilitate the process of establishing associative links needed for consolidation of vocabulary
- You can estimate the number of learned words and hence your level of language knowledge
- The dictionary allows for the creation of an effective and high-quality revision process
- You can revise certain themes several times, modifying the revision methods and techniques
- Audio versions of the dictionaries help you to work out the pronunciation of words and develop your skills of auditory word perception

The T&P Books' theme-based dictionaries are offered in several variants differing in the number of words: 1.500, 3.000, 5.000, 7.000, and 9.000 words. There are also dictionaries containing 15,000 words for some language combinations. Your choice of dictionary will depend on your knowledge level and goals.

We sincerely believe that our dictionaries will become your trusty assistant in learning foreign languages and will allow you to easily acquire the necessary vocabulary.

TABLE OF CONTENTS

PRONUNCIATION GUIDE

T&P phonetic alphabet	Kyrgyz example	English example
[a]	манжа [mandʒa]	shorter than in ask
[e]	келечек [keletʃek]	elm, medal
[i]	жигит [dʒigit]	shorter than in feet
[ɪ]	кубаныч [kubanɪtʃ]	big, America
[o]	мактоо [maktoo]	pod, John
[u]	узундук [uzunduk]	book
[ʉ]	алюминий [alʉminij]	youth, usually
[y]	түнкү [tynky]	fuel, tuna
[b]	ашкабак [aʃkabak]	baby, book
[d]	адам [adam]	day, doctor
[dʒ]	жыгач [dʒɪgatʃ]	joke, general
[f]	флейта [flejta]	face, food
[g]	тегерек [tegerek]	game, gold
[j]	бөйрөк [bøjrøk]	yes, New York
[k]	карапа [karapa]	clock, kiss
[l]	алтын [altɪn]	lace, people
[m]	бешмант [beʃmant]	magic, milk
[n]	найза [najza]	name, normal
[ŋ]	булуң [buluŋ]	ring
[p]	пайдубал [pajdubal]	pencil, private
[r]	рахмат [raχmat]	rice, radio
[s]	сагызган [sagɪzgan]	city, boss
[ʃ]	бурулуш [buruluʃ]	machine, shark
[t]	түтүн [tytyn]	tourist, trip
[χ]	пахтадан [paχtadan]	hot, hobby
[ts]	шприц [ʃprits]	cats, tsetse fly
[tʃ]	биринчи [birintʃi]	church, French
[v]	квартал [kvartal]	very, river
[z]	казуу [kazuu]	zebra, please
[ʲ]	руль, актёр [rulʲ, aktʲor]	palatalization sign

ABBREVIATIONS
used in the vocabulary

English abbreviations

ab.	-	about
adj	-	adjective
adv	-	adverb
anim.	-	animate
as adj	-	attributive noun used as adjective
e.g.	-	for example
etc.	-	et cetera
fam.	-	familiar
fem.	-	feminine
form.	-	formal
inanim.	-	inanimate
masc.	-	masculine
math	-	mathematics
mil.	-	military
n	-	noun
pl	-	plural
pron.	-	pronoun
sb	-	somebody
sing.	-	singular
sth	-	something
v aux	-	auxiliary verb
vi	-	intransitive verb
vi, vt	-	intransitive, transitive verb
vt	-	transitive verb

BASIC CONCEPTS

1. Pronouns

I, me	мен, мага	men, maga
you	сен	sen
he, she, it	ал	al
we	биз	biz
you (to a group)	силер	siler
you (polite, sing.)	сиз	siz
you (polite, pl)	сиздер	sizder
they	алар	alar

2. Greetings. Salutations

Hello! (fam.)	Салам!	salam!
Hello! (form.)	Саламатсызбы!	salamatsızbı!
Good morning!	Кутман таңыңыз менен!	kutman taŋıŋız menen!
Good afternoon!	Кутман күнүңүз менен!	kutman kynyŋyz menen!
Good evening!	Кутман кечиңиз менен!	kutman ketʃiŋiz menen!
to say hello	учурашуу	utʃuraʃuu
Hi! (hello)	Кандай!	kandaj!
greeting (n)	салам	salam
to greet (vt)	саламдашуу	salamdaʃuu
How are you?	Иштериң кандай?	iʃteriŋ kandaj?
How are you? (form.)	Иштериңиз кандай?	iʃteriŋiz kandaj?
How are you? (fam.)	Иштер кандай?	iʃter kandaj?
What's new?	Эмне жаңылык?	emne dʒaŋılık?
Bye-Bye! Goodbye!	Көрүшкөнчө!	køryʃkøntʃø!
See you soon!	Эмки жолукканга чейин!	emki dʒolukkanga tʃejin!
Farewell! (to a friend)	Кош бол!	koʃ bol!
Farewell! (form.)	кырк бир	kırk bir
to say goodbye	коштошуу	koʃtoʃuu
So long!	Жакшы кал!	dʒakʃı kal!
Thank you!	Рахмат!	raχmat!
Thank you very much!	Чоң рахмат!	tʃoŋ raχmat!
You're welcome	Эч нерсе эмес	etʃ nerse emes
Don't mention it!	Алкышка арзыбайт	alkıʃka arzıbajt
It was nothing	Эчтеке эмес.	etʃteke emes

Excuse me! (fam.)	Кечир!	ketʃir!
Excuse me! (form.)	Кечирип коюнузчу!	ketʃirip kojɯŋuztʃu!
to excuse (forgive)	кечирүү	ketʃiryy

to apologize (vi)	кечирим суроо	ketʃirim suroo
My apologies	Кечирим сурайм.	ketʃirim surajm
I'm sorry!	Кечиресиз!	ketʃiresiz!
to forgive (vt)	кечирүү	ketʃiryy
It's okay! (that's all right)	Эч капачылык жок.	etʃ kapatʃɯlɯk dʒok
please (adv)	суранам	suranam

Don't forget!	Унутуп калбаңыз!	unutup kalbaŋɯz!
Certainly!	Албетте!	albette!
Of course not!	Албетте жок!	albette dʒok!
Okay! (I agree)	Макул!	makul!
That's enough!	Жетишет!	dʒetiʃet!

3. Questions

Who?	Ким?	kim?
What?	Эмне?	emne?
Where? (at, in)	Каерде?	kaerde?
Where (to)?	Каяка?	kajaka?
From where?	Каяктан?	kajaktan?
When?	Качан?	katʃan?
Why? (What for?)	Эмне үчүн?	emne ytʃyn?
Why? (~ are you crying?)	Эмнеге?	emnege?

What for?	Кайсы керекке?	kajsɯ kerekke?
How? (in what way)	Кандай?	kandaj?
What? (What kind of ...?)	Кайсы?	kajsɯ?
Which?	Кайсынысы?	kajsɯnɯsɯ?

To whom?	Кимге?	kimge?
About whom?	Ким жөнүндө?	kim dʒønyndø?
About what?	Эмне жөнүндө?	emne dʒønyndø?
With whom?	Ким менен?	kim menen?

How many? How much?	Канча?	kantʃa?
Whose?	Кимдики?	kimdiki?
Whose? (fem.)	Кимдики?	kimdiki?
Whose? (pl)	Кимдердики?	kimderdiki?

4. Prepositions

with (accompanied by)	менен	menen
without	-сыз, -сиз	-sɯz, -siz
to (indicating direction)	... көздөй	... køzdøj

about (talking ~ ...)	... жөнүндө	... dʒønyndø
before (in time)	... астында	... astında
in front of ...	... алдында	... aldında

under (beneath, below)	... астында	... astında
above (over)	... өйдө	... øjdø
on (atop)	... үстүндө	... ystyndø
from (off, out of)	-дан	-dan
of (made from)	-дан	-dan

| in (e.g., ~ ten minutes) | ... ичинде | ... itʃinde |
| over (across the top of) | ... үстүнөн | ... ystynøn |

5. Function words. Adverbs. Part 1

Where? (at, in)	**Каерде?**	kaerde?
here (adv)	**бул жерде**	bul dʒerde
there (adv)	**тээтигил жакта**	teetigil dʒakta

| somewhere (to be) | **бир жерде** | bir dʒerde |
| nowhere (not in any place) | **эч жакта** | etʃ dʒakta |

| by (near, beside) | **... жанында** | ... dʒanında |
| by the window | **терезенин жанында** | terezenin dʒanında |

Where (to)?	**Каяка?**	kajaka?
here (e.g., come ~!)	**бери**	beri
there (e.g., to go ~)	**нары**	narı
from here (adv)	**бул жерден**	bul dʒerden
from there (adv)	**тигил жерден**	tigil dʒerden

| close (adv) | **жакын** | dʒakın |
| far (adv) | **алыс** | alıs |

near (e.g., ~ Paris)	**... тегерегинде**	... tegereginde
nearby (adv)	**жакын арада**	dʒakın arada
not far (adv)	**алыс эмес**	alıs emes

left (adj)	**сол**	sol
on the left	**сол жакта**	sol dʒakta
to the left	**солго**	solgo

right (adj)	**оң**	oŋ
on the right	**оң жакта**	oŋ dʒakta
to the right	**оңго**	oŋgo

in front (adv)	**астыда**	astıda
front (as adj)	**алдыңкы**	aldıŋkı
ahead (the kids ran ~)	**алдыга**	aldıga
behind (adv)	**артында**	artında

| from behind | **артынан** | artınan |
| back (towards the rear) | **артка** | artka |

| middle | **ортосу** | ortosu |
| in the middle | **ортосунда** | ortosunda |

at the side	**капталында**	kaptalında
everywhere (adv)	**бүт жерде**	byt dʒerde
around (in all directions)	**айланасында**	ajlanasında

from inside	**ичинде**	itʃinde
somewhere (to go)	**бир жерде**	bir dʒerde
straight (directly)	**түз**	tyz
back (e.g., come ~)	**кайра**	kajra

| from anywhere | **бир жерден** | bir dʒerden |
| from somewhere | **бир жактан** | bir dʒaktan |

firstly (adv)	**биринчиден**	birintʃiden
secondly (adv)	**экинчиден**	ekintʃiden
thirdly (adv)	**үчүнчүдөн**	ytʃyntʃydøn

suddenly (adv)	**күтпөгөн жерден**	kytpøgøn dʒerden
at first (in the beginning)	**башында**	baʃında
for the first time	**биринчи жолу**	birintʃi dʒolu
long before ...	**... алдында**	... aldında
anew (over again)	**башынан**	baʃınan
for good (adv)	**түбөлүккө**	tybølykkø

never (adv)	**эч качан**	etʃ katʃan
again (adv)	**кайра**	kajra
now (at present)	**эми**	emi
often (adv)	**көпчүлүк учурда**	køptʃylyk utʃurda
then (adv)	**анда**	anda
urgently (quickly)	**тезинен**	tezinen
usually (adv)	**көбүнчө**	købyntʃø

by the way, ...	**баса, ...**	basa, ...
possibly	**мүмкүн**	mymkyn
probably (adv)	**балким**	balkim
maybe (adv)	**ыктымал**	ıktımal
besides ...	**андан тышкары, ...**	andan tıʃkarı, ...
that's why ...	**ошондуктан ...**	oʃonduktan ...
in spite of ...	**... карабастан**	... karabastan
thanks to ...	**... күчү менен**	... kytʃy menen

what (pron.)	**эмне**	emne
that (conj.)	**эмне**	emne
something	**бир нерсе**	bir nerse
anything (something)	**бир нерсе**	bir nerse
nothing	**эч нерсе**	etʃ nerse
who (pron.)	**ким**	kim

someone	кимдир бирөө	kimdir birøø
somebody	бирөө жарым	birøø dʒarım
nobody	эч ким	etʃ kim
nowhere (a voyage to ~)	эч жака	etʃ dʒaka
nobody's	эч кимдики	etʃ kimdiki
somebody's	бирөөнүкү	birøønyky
so (I'm ~ glad)	эми	emi
also (as well)	ошондой эле	oʃondoj ele
too (as well)	дагы	dagı

6. Function words. Adverbs. Part 2

Why?	Эмнеге?	emnege?
for some reason	эмнегедир	emnegedir
because ...	... себептен	... sebepten
for some purpose	эмне үчүндүр	emne ytʃyndyr
and	жана	dʒana
or	же	dʒe
but	бирок	birok
for (e.g., ~ me)	үчүн	ytʃyn
too (~ many people)	өтө эле	øtø ele
only (exclusively)	азыр эле	azır ele
exactly (adv)	так	tak
about (more or less)	болжол менен	boldʒol menen
approximately (adv)	болжол менен	boldʒol menen
approximate (adj)	болжолдуу	boldʒolduu
almost (adv)	дээрлик	deerlik
the rest	калганы	kalganı
the other (second)	башка	baʃka
other (different)	башка бөлөк	baʃka bøløk
each (adj)	ар бири	ar biri
any (no matter which)	баардык	baardık
many, much (a lot of)	көп	køp
many people	көбү	køby
all (everyone)	баары	baarı
in return for ...	... алмашуу	... almaʃuu
in exchange (adv)	ордуна	orduna
by hand (made)	колго	kolgo
hardly (negative opinion)	ишенүүгө болбойт	iʃenyygø bolbojt
probably (adv)	балким	balkim
on purpose (intentionally)	атайын	atajın
by accident (adv)	кокустан	kokustan

very (adv)	**аябай**	ajabaj
for example (adv)	**мисалы**	misalı
between	**ортосунда**	ortosunda
among	**арасында**	arasında
so much (such a lot)	**ошончо**	oʃontʃo
especially (adv)	**өзгөчө**	øzgøtʃø

NUMBERS. MISCELLANEOUS

7. Cardinal numbers. Part 1

0 zero	нөл	nøl
1 one	бир	bir
2 two	эки	eki
3 three	үч	ytʃ
4 four	төрт	tørt
5 five	беш	beʃ
6 six	алты	altı
7 seven	жети	dʒeti
8 eight	сегиз	segiz
9 nine	тогуз	toguz
10 ten	он	on
11 eleven	он бир	on bir
12 twelve	он эки	on eki
13 thirteen	он үч	on ytʃ
14 fourteen	он төрт	on tørt
15 fifteen	он беш	on beʃ
16 sixteen	он алты	on altı
17 seventeen	он жети	on dʒeti
18 eighteen	он сегиз	on segiz
19 nineteen	он тогуз	on toguz
20 twenty	жыйырма	dʒıjırma
21 twenty-one	жыйырма бир	dʒıjırma bir
22 twenty-two	жыйырма эки	dʒıjırma eki
23 twenty-three	жыйырма үч	dʒıjırma ytʃ
30 thirty	отуз	otuz
31 thirty-one	отуз бир	otuz bir
32 thirty-two	отуз эки	otuz eki
33 thirty-three	отуз үч	otuz ytʃ
40 forty	кырк	kırk
42 forty-two	кырк эки	kırk eki
43 forty-three	кырк үч	kırk ytʃ
50 fifty	элүү	elyy
51 fifty-one	элүү бир	elyy bir
52 fifty-two	элүү эки	elyy eki
53 fifty-three	элүү үч	elyy ytʃ

60 sixty	алтымыш	altımıʃ
61 sixty-one	алтымыш бир	altımıʃ bir
62 sixty-two	алтымыш эки	altımıʃ eki
63 sixty-three	алтымыш үч	altımıʃ ytʃ
70 seventy	жетимиш	dʒetimiʃ
71 seventy-one	жетимиш бир	dʒetimiʃ bir
72 seventy-two	жетимиш эки	dʒetimiʃ eki
73 seventy-three	жетимиш үч	dʒetimiʃ ytʃ
80 eighty	сексен	seksen
81 eighty-one	сексен бир	seksen bir
82 eighty-two	сексен эки	seksen eki
83 eighty-three	сексен үч	seksen ytʃ
90 ninety	токсон	tokson
91 ninety-one	токсон бир	tokson bir
92 ninety-two	токсон эки	tokson eki
93 ninety-three	токсон үч	tokson ytʃ

8. Cardinal numbers. Part 2

100 one hundred	бир жүз	bir dʒyz
200 two hundred	эки жүз	eki dʒyz
300 three hundred	үч жүз	ytʃ dʒyz
400 four hundred	төрт жүз	tørt dʒyz
500 five hundred	беш жүз	beʃ dʒyz
600 six hundred	алты жүз	altı dʒyz
700 seven hundred	жети жүз	dʒeti dʒyz
800 eight hundred	сегиз жүз	segiz dʒyz
900 nine hundred	тогуз жүз	toguz dʒyz
1000 one thousand	бир миң	bir miŋ
2000 two thousand	эки миң	eki miŋ
3000 three thousand	үч миң	ytʃ miŋ
10000 ten thousand	он миң	on miŋ
one hundred thousand	жүз миң	dʒyz miŋ
million	миллион	million
billion	миллиард	milliard

9. Ordinal numbers

first (adj)	биринчи	birintʃi
second (adj)	экинчи	ekintʃi
third (adj)	үчүнчү	ytʃyntʃy
fourth (adj)	төртүнчү	tørtyntʃy
fifth (adj)	бешинчи	beʃintʃi

sixth (adj)	алтынчы	altıntʃı
seventh (adj)	жетинчи	dʒetintʃi
eighth (adj)	сегизинчи	segizintʃi
ninth (adj)	тогузунчу	toguzuntʃu
tenth (adj)	онунчу	onuntʃu

COLOURS. UNITS OF MEASUREMENT

10. Colors

color	түс	tys
shade (tint)	кошумча түс	koʃumʧa tys
hue	кубулуу	kubuluu
rainbow	күндүн кулагы	kyndyn kulagı
white (adj)	ак	ak
black (adj)	кара	kara
gray (adj)	боз	boz
green (adj)	жашыл	ʤaʃıl
yellow (adj)	сары	sarı
red (adj)	кызыл	kızıl
blue (adj)	көк	køk
light blue (adj)	көгүлтүр	køgyltyr
pink (adj)	мала	mala
orange (adj)	кызгылт сары	kızgılt sarı
violet (adj)	сыя көк	sıja køk
brown (adj)	күрөң	kyrøŋ
golden (adj)	алтын түстүү	altın tystyy
silvery (adj)	күмүш өңдүү	kymyʃ øŋdyy
beige (adj)	сары боз	sarı boz
cream (adj)	саргылт	sargılt
turquoise (adj)	бирюза	birɯza
cherry red (adj)	кочкул кызыл	kotʃkul kızıl
lilac (adj)	кызгылт көгүш	kızgılt køgyʃ
crimson (adj)	ачык кызыл	atʃık kızıl
light (adj)	ачык	atʃık
dark (adj)	күңүрт	kyŋyrt
bright, vivid (adj)	ачык	atʃık
colored (pencils)	түстүү	tystyy
color (e.g., ~ film)	түстүү	tystyy
black-and-white (adj)	ак-кара	ak-kara
plain (one-colored)	бир өңчөй түстө	bir øŋʧøj tystø
multicolored (adj)	ар түрдүү түстө	ar tyrdyy tystø

11. Units of measurement

weight	салмак	salmak
length	узундук	uzunduk
width	жазылык	dʒazılık
height	бийиктик	bijiktik
depth	терендик	terendik
volume	көлөм	køløm
area	аянт	ajant
gram	грамм	gramm
milligram	миллиграмм	milligramm
kilogram	килограмм	kilogramm
ton	тонна	tonna
pound	фунт	funt
ounce	унция	untsija
meter	метр	metr
millimeter	миллиметр	millimetr
centimeter	сантиметр	santimetr
kilometer	километр	kilometr
mile	миля	milʲa
inch	дюйм	dʉjm
foot	фут	fut
yard	ярд	jard
square meter	квадраттык метр	kvadrattık metr
hectare	гектар	gektar
liter	литр	litr
degree	градус	gradus
volt	вольт	volʲt
ampere	ампер	amper
horsepower	ат күчү	at kytʃy
quantity	саны	sanı
a little bit of ...	... бир аз	... bir az
half	жарым	dʒarım
dozen	он эки даана	on eki daana
piece (item)	даана	daana
size	чондук	tʃonduk
scale (map ~)	өлчөмчен	øltʃømtʃen
minimal (adj)	минималдуу	minimalduu
the smallest (adj)	эң кичинекей	eŋ kitʃinekej
medium (adj)	орточо	ortotʃo
maximal (adj)	максималдуу	maksimalduu
the largest (adj)	эң чоң	eŋ tʃoŋ

12. Containers

canning jar (glass ~)	банка	banka
can	банка	banka
bucket	чака	ʧaka
barrel	бочка	boʧka

wash basin (e.g., plastic ~)	дагара	dagara
tank (100L water ~)	бак	bak
hip flask	фляжка	flʲadʒka
jerrycan	канистра	kanistra
tank (e.g., tank car)	цистерна	ʦɪsterna

mug	кружка	krudʒka
cup (of coffee, etc.)	чөйчөк	ʧøjʧøk
saucer	табак	tabak
glass (tumbler)	ыстакан	ɪstakan
wine glass	бокал	bokal
stock pot (soup pot)	мискей	miskej

bottle (~ of wine)	бөтөлкө	bøtølkø
neck (of the bottle, etc.)	оозу	oozu

carafe (decanter)	графин	grafin
pitcher	кумура	kumura
vessel (container)	идиш	idiʃ
pot (crock, stoneware ~)	карапа	karapa
vase	ваза	vaza

flacon, bottle (perfume ~)	флакон	flakon
vial, small bottle	кичине бөтөлкө	kitʃine bøtølkø
tube (of toothpaste)	түбик	tʉbik

sack (bag)	кап	kap
bag (paper ~, plastic ~)	пакет	paket
pack (of cigarettes, etc.)	пачке	paʧke

box (e.g., shoebox)	куту	kutu
crate	үкөк	ykøk
basket	себет	sebet

MAIN VERBS

13. The most important verbs. Part 1

to advise (vt)	кеңеш берүү	keŋeʃ beryy
to agree (say yes)	макул болуу	makul boluu
to answer (vi, vt)	жооп берүү	dʒoop beryy
to apologize (vi)	кечирим суроо	ketʃirim suroo
to arrive (vi)	келүү	kelyy
to ask (~ oneself)	суроо	suroo
to ask (~ sb to do sth)	суроо	suroo
to be (vi)	болуу	boluu
to be afraid	жазкануу	dʒazkanuu
to be hungry	ачка болуу	atʃka boluu
to be interested in ...	... кызыгуу	... kızıguu
to be needed	керек болуу	kerek boluu
to be surprised	таң калуу	taŋ kaluu
to be thirsty	суусап калуу	suusap kaluu
to begin (vt)	баштоо	baʃtoo
to belong to ...	таандык болуу	taandık boluu
to boast (vi)	мактануу	maktanuu
to break (split into pieces)	сындыруу	sındıruu
to call (~ for help)	чакыруу	tʃakıruu
can (v aux)	жасай алуу	dʒasaj aluu
to catch (vt)	кармоо	karmoo
to change (vt)	өзгөртүү	øzgørtyy
to choose (select)	тандоо	tandoo
to come down (the stairs)	ылдый түшүү	ıldıj tyʃyy
to compare (vt)	салыштыруу	salıʃtıruu
to complain (vi, vt)	арыздануу	arızdanuu
to confuse (mix up)	адаштыруу	adaʃtıruu
to continue (vt)	улантуу	ulantuu
to control (vt)	башкаруу	baʃkaruu
to cook (dinner)	тамак бышыруу	tamak bıʃıruu
to cost (vt)	туруу	turuu
to count (add up)	саноо	sanoo
to count on ...	... ишенүү	... iʃenyy
to create (vt)	жаратуу	dʒaratuu
to cry (weep)	ыйлоо	ıjloo

14. The most important verbs. Part 2

to deceive (vi, vt)	алдоо	aldoo
to decorate (tree, street)	кооздоо	koozdoo
to defend (a country, etc.)	коргоо	korgoo
to demand (request firmly)	талап кылуу	talap kıluu
to dig (vt)	казуу	kazuu

to discuss (vt)	талкуулоо	talkuuloo
to do (vt)	кылуу	kıluu
to doubt (have doubts)	күмөн саноо	kymөn sanoo
to drop (let fall)	түшүрүп алуу	tyʃyryp aluu
to enter (room, house, etc.)	кирүү	kiryy

to excuse (forgive)	кечирүү	ketʃiryy
to exist (vi)	чыгуу	tʃıguu
to expect (foresee)	күтүү	kytyy
to explain (vt)	түшүндүрүү	tyʃyndyryy
to fall (vi)	жыгылуу	dʒıgıluu

to find (vt)	таап алуу	taap aluu
to finish (vt)	бүтүрүү	bytyryy
to fly (vi)	учуу	utʃuu

| to follow … (come after) | … ээрчүү | … eertʃyy |
| to forget (vi, vt) | унутуу | unutuu |

| to forgive (vt) | кечирүү | ketʃiryy |
| to give (vt) | берүү | beryy |

| to give a hint | четин чыгаруу | tʃetin tʃıgaruu |
| to go (on foot) | жөө басуу | dʒөө basuu |

to go for a swim	сууга түшүү	suuga tyʃyy
to go out (for dinner, etc.)	чыгуу	tʃıguu
to guess (the answer)	жандырмагын табуу	dʒandırmagın tabuu

| to have (vt) | бар болуу | bar boluu |
| to have breakfast | эртең менен тамактануу | erteŋ menen tamaktanuu |

| to have dinner | кечки тамакты ичүү | ketʃki tamaktı itʃyy |

| to have lunch | түштөнүү | tyʃtөnyy |
| to hear (vt) | угуу | uguu |

to help (vt)	жардам берүү	dʒardam beryy
to hide (vt)	жашыруу	dʒaʃıruu
to hope (vi, vt)	үмүттөнүү	ymyttөnyy
to hunt (vi, vt)	аңчылык кылуу	aŋtʃılık kıluu
to hurry (vi)	шашуу	ʃaʃuu

15. The most important verbs. Part 3

to inform (vt)	маалымат берүү	maalımat beryy
to insist (vi, vt)	көшөрүү	køʃøryy
to insult (vt)	кемсинтүү	kemsintyy
to invite (vt)	чакыруу	tʃakıruu
to joke (vi)	тамашалоо	tamaʃaloo
to keep (vt)	сактоо	saktoo
to keep silent, to hush	унчукпоо	untʃukpoo
to kill (vt)	өлтүрүү	øltyryy
to know (sb)	таануу	taanuu
to know (sth)	билүү	bilyy
to laugh (vi)	күлүү	kylyy
to liberate (city, etc.)	бошотуу	boʃotuu
to like (I like …)	жактыруу	dʒaktıruu
to look for … (search)	… издөө	… izdøø
to love (sb)	сүйүү	syjyy
to make a mistake	ката кетирүү	kata ketiryy
to manage, to run	башкаруу	baʃkaruu
to mean (signify)	билдирүү	bildiryy
to mention (talk about)	айтып өтүү	ajtıp øtyy
to miss (school, etc.)	калтыруу	kaltıruu
to notice (see)	байкоо	bajkoo
to object (vi, vt)	каршы болуу	karʃı boluu
to observe (see)	байкоо салуу	bajkoo
to open (vt)	ачуу	atʃuu
to order (meal, etc.)	буйрутма кылуу	bujrutma kıluu
to order (mil.)	буйрук кылуу	bujruk kıluu
to own (possess)	ээ болуу	ee boluu
to participate (vi)	катышуу	katıʃuu
to pay (vi, vt)	төлөө	tøløø
to permit (vt)	уруксат берүү	uruksat beryy
to plan (vt)	пландаштыруу	plandaʃtıruu
to play (children)	ойноо	ojnoo
to pray (vi, vt)	дуба кылуу	duba kıluu
to prefer (vt)	артык көрүү	artık køryy
to promise (vt)	убада берүү	ubada beryy
to pronounce (vt)	айтуу	ajtuu
to propose (vt)	сунуштоо	sunuʃtoo
to punish (vt)	жазалоо	dʒazaloo

16. The most important verbs. Part 4

to read (vi, vt)	окуу	okuu
to recommend (vt)	сунуштоо	sunuʃtoo

to refuse (vi, vt)	баш тартуу	baʃ tartuu
to regret (be sorry)	өкүнүү	økynyy
to rent (sth from sb)	батирге алуу	batirge aluu
to repeat (say again)	кайталоо	kajtaloo
to reserve, to book	камдык буйрутмалоо	kamdık bujrutmaloo
to run (vi)	чуркоо	tʃurkoo
to save (rescue)	куткаруу	kutkaruu
to say (~ thank you)	айтуу	ajtuu
to scold (vt)	урушуу	uruʃuu
to see (vt)	көрүү	køryy
to sell (vt)	сатуу	satuu
to send (vt)	жөнөтүү	dʒønøtyy
to shoot (vi)	атуу	atuu
to shout (vi)	кыйкыруу	kıjkıruu
to show (vt)	көрсөтүү	kørsøtyy
to sign (document)	кол коюу	kol kojuu
to sit down (vi)	отуруу	oturuu
to smile (vi)	жылмаюу	dʒılmadʒuu
to speak (vi, vt)	сүйлөө	syjløø
to steal (money, etc.)	уурдоо	uurdoo
to stop (for pause, etc.)	токтоо	toktoo
to stop (please ~ calling me)	токтотуу	toktotuu
to study (vt)	окуу	okuu
to swim (vi)	сүзүү	syzyy
to take (vt)	алуу	aluu
to think (vi, vt)	ойлоо	ojloo
to threaten (vt)	коркутуу	korkutuu
to touch (with hands)	тийүү	tijyy
to translate (vt)	которуу	kotoruu
to trust (vt)	ишенүү	iʃenyy
to try (attempt)	аракет кылуу	araket kıluu
to turn (e.g., ~ left)	бурулуу	buruluu
to underestimate (vt)	баалабоо	baalaboo
to understand (vt)	түшүнүү	tyʃynyy
to unite (vt)	бириктирүү	biriktiryy
to wait (vt)	күтүү	kytyy
to want (wish, desire)	каалоо	kaaloo
to warn (vt)	эскертүү	eskertyy
to work (vi)	иштөө	iʃtøø
to write (vt)	жазуу	dʒazuu
to write down	кагазга түшүрүү	kagazga tyʃyryy

TIME. CALENDAR

17. Weekdays

Monday	дүйшөмбү	dyjʃømby
Tuesday	шейшемби	ʃejʃembi
Wednesday	шаршемби	ʃarʃembi
Thursday	бейшемби	bejʃembi
Friday	жума	dʒuma
Saturday	ишенби	iʃenbi
Sunday	жекшемби	dʒekʃembi
today (adv)	бүгүн	bygyn
tomorrow (adv)	эртең	erteŋ
the day after tomorrow	бирсүгүнү	birsygyny
yesterday (adv)	кечээ	ketʃee
the day before yesterday	мурда күнү	murda kyny
day	күн	kyn
working day	иш күнү	iʃ kyny
public holiday	майрам күнү	majram kyny
day off	дем алыш күн	dem alıʃ kyn
weekend	дем алыш күндөр	dem alıʃ kyndør
all day long	күнү бою	kyny bojʉ
the next day (adv)	кийинки күнү	kijinki kyny
two days ago	эки күн мурун	eki kyn murun
the day before	жакында	dʒakında
daily (adj)	күндө	kyndø
every day (adv)	күн сайын	kyn sajın
week	жума	dʒuma
last week (adv)	өткөн жумада	øtkøn dʒumada
next week (adv)	келаткан жумада	kelatkan dʒumada
weekly (adj)	жума сайын	dʒuma sajın
every week (adv)	жума сайын	dʒuma sajın
twice a week	жумасына эки жолу	dʒumasına eki dʒolu
every Tuesday	ар шейшемби	ar ʃejʃembi

18. Hours. Day and night

morning	таң	taŋ
in the morning	эртең менен	erteŋ menen
noon, midday	жарым күн	dʒarım kyn

in the afternoon	түштөн кийин	tyʃtøn kijin
evening	кеч	ketʃ
in the evening	кечинде	ketʃinde
night	түн	tyn
at night	түндө	tyndø
midnight	жарым түн	dʒarım tyn

second	секунда	sekunda
minute	мүнөт	mynøt
hour	саат	saat
half an hour	жарым саат	dʒarım saat
a quarter-hour	чейрек саат	tʃejrek saat
fifteen minutes	он беш мүнөт	on beʃ mynøt
24 hours	сутка	sutka

sunrise	күндүн чыгышы	kyndyn tʃıgıʃı
dawn	таң агаруу	taŋ agaruu
early morning	таң эрте	taŋ erte
sunset	күн батуу	kyn batuu

early in the morning	таң эрте	taŋ erte
this morning	бүгүн эртең менен	bygyn erteŋ menen
tomorrow morning	эртең эртең менен	erteŋ erteŋ menen

this afternoon	күндүзү	kyndyzy
in the afternoon	түштөн кийин	tyʃtøn kijin
tomorrow afternoon	эртең түштөн кийин	erteŋ tyʃtøn kijin

tonight (this evening)	бүгүн кечинде	bygyn ketʃinde
tomorrow night	эртең кечинде	erteŋ ketʃinde

at 3 o'clock sharp	туура саат үчтө	tuura saat ytʃtø
about 4 o'clock	болжол менен төрт саат	boldʒol menen tørt saat
by 12 o'clock	саат он экиде	saat on ekide

in 20 minutes	жыйырма мүнөттөн кийин	dʒıjırma mynøttøn kijin
in an hour	бир сааттан кийин	bir saattan kijin
on time (adv)	өз убагында	øz ubagında

a quarter to ...	... он беш мүнөт калды	... on beʃ mynøt kaldı
within an hour	бир сааттын ичинде	bir saattın itʃinde
every 15 minutes	он беш мүнөт сайын	on beʃ mynøt sajın
round the clock	бир сутка бою	bir sutka bojʉ

19. Months. Seasons

January	январь	janvarʲ
February	февраль	fevralʲ

March	март	mart
April	апрель	aprelʲ
May	май	maj
June	июнь	ijʉnʲ
July	июль	ijʉlʲ
August	август	avgust
September	сентябрь	sentʲabrʲ
October	октябрь	oktʲabrʲ
November	ноябрь	nojabrʲ
December	декабрь	dekabrʲ
spring	жаз	dʒaz
in spring	жазында	dʒazında
spring (as adj)	жазгы	dʒazgı
summer	жай	dʒaj
in summer	жайында	dʒajında
summer (as adj)	жайкы	dʒajkı
fall	күз	kyz
in fall	күзүндө	kyzyndø
fall (as adj)	күздүк	kyzdyk
winter	кыш	kıʃ
in winter	кышында	kıʃinda
winter (as adj)	кышкы	kıʃkı
month	ай	aj
this month	ушул айда	uʃul ajda
next month	кийинки айда	kijinki ajda
last month	өткөн айда	øtkøn ajda
a month ago	бир ай мурун	bir aj murun
in a month (a month later)	бир айдан кийин	bir ajdan kijin
in 2 months (2 months later)	эки айдан кийин	eki ajdan kijin
the whole month	ай бою	aj bojʉ
all month long	толук бир ай	toluk bir aj
monthly (~ magazine)	ай сайын	aj sajın
monthly (adv)	ай сайын	aj sajın
every month	ар бир айда	ar bir ajda
twice a month	айына эки жолу	ajına eki dʒolu
year	жыл	dʒıl
this year	бул жылы	bul dʒılı
next year	келаткан жылы	kelatkan dʒılı
last year	өткөн жылы	øtkøn dʒılı
a year ago	бир жыл мурун	bir dʒıl murun
in a year	бир жылдан кийин	bir dʒıldan kijin

in two years	эки жылдан кийин	eki ʤıldan kijin
the whole year	жыл бою	ʤıl boʤʉ
all year long	толук бир жыл	toluk bir ʤıl
every year	ар жыл сайын	ar ʤıl sajın
annual (adj)	жыл сайын	ʤıl sajın
annually (adv)	жыл сайын	ʤıl sajın
4 times a year	жылына төрт жолу	ʤılına tørt ʤolu
date (e.g., today's ~)	число	ʧislo
date (e.g., ~ of birth)	күн	kyn
calendar	календарь	kalendarʲ
half a year	жарым жыл	ʤarım ʤıl
six months	жарым чейрек	ʤarım ʧejrek
season (summer, etc.)	мезгил	mezgil
century	кылым	kılım

TRAVEL. HOTEL

20. Trip. Travel

tourism, travel	туризм	turizm
tourist	турист	turist
trip, voyage	саякат	sajakat
adventure	укмуштуу окуя	ukmuʃtuu okuja
trip, journey	сапар	sapar
vacation	дем алыш	dem alıʃ
to be on vacation	дем алышка чыгуу	dem alıʃka ʧıguu
rest	эс алуу	es aluu
train	поезд	poezd
by train	поезд менен	poezd menen
airplane	учак	uʧak
by airplane	учакта	uʧakta
by car	автомобилде	avtomobilde
by ship	кемеде	kemede
luggage	жүк	ʤyk
suitcase	чемодан	ʧemodan
luggage cart	араба	araba
passport	паспорт	pasport
visa	виза	viza
ticket	билет	bilet
air ticket	авиабилет	aviabilet
guidebook	жол көрсөткүч	ʤol kørsøtkyʧ
map (tourist ~)	карта	karta
area (rural ~)	жай	ʤaj
place, site	жер	ʤer
exotica (n)	экзотика	ekzotika
exotic (adj)	экзотикалуу	ekzotikaluu
amazing (adj)	ажайып	aʤajıp
group	топ	top
excursion, sightseeing tour	экскурсия	ekskursija
guide (person)	экскурсия жетекчиси	ekskursija ʤetekʧisi

21. Hotel

hotel, inn	мейманкана	mejmankana
motel	мотель	motelʲ
three-star (~ hotel)	үч жылдыздуу	ytʃ dʒıldızduu
five-star	беш жылдыздуу	beʃ dʒıldızduu
to stay (in a hotel, etc.)	токтоо	toktoo
room	номер	nomer
single room	бир орундуу	bir orunduu
double room	эки орундуу	eki orunduu
to book a room	номерди камдык буйрутмалоо	nomerdi kamdık bujrutmaloo
half board	жарым пансион	dʒarım pansion
full board	толук пансион	toluk pansion
with bath	ваннасы менен	vannası menen
with shower	душ менен	duʃ menen
satellite television	спутник	sputnik
air-conditioner	аба желдеткич	aba dʒeldetkitʃ
towel	сүлгү	sylgy
key	ачкыч	atʃkıtʃ
administrator	администратор	administrator
chambermaid	үй кызматкери	yj kızmatkeri
porter, bellboy	жүк ташуучу	dʒyk taʃuutʃu
doorman	эшик ачуучу	eʃik atʃuutʃu
restaurant	ресторан	restoran
pub, bar	бар	bar
breakfast	таңкы тамак	taŋkı tamak
dinner	кечки тамак	ketʃki tamak
buffet	шведче стол	ʃvedtʃe stol
lobby	вестибюль	vestibulʲ
elevator	лифт	lift
DO NOT DISTURB	ТЫНЧЫБЫЗДЫ АЛБАГЫЛА!	tıntʃıbızdı albagıla!
NO SMOKING	ТАМЕКИ ЧЕГҮҮГӨ БОЛБОЙТ!	tameki tʃegyygø bolbojt!

22. Sightseeing

monument	эстелик	estelik
fortress	чеп	tʃep
palace	сарай	saraj

castle	сепил	sepil
tower	мунара	munara
mausoleum	күмбөз	kymbøz

architecture	архитектура	arχitektura
medieval (adj)	орто кылымдык	orto kılımdık
ancient (adj)	байыркы	bajırkı
national (adj)	улуттук	uluttuk
famous (monument, etc.)	таанымал	taanımal

tourist	турист	turist
guide (person)	гид	gid
excursion, sightseeing tour	экскурсия	ekskursija
to show (vt)	көрсөтүү	kørsøtyy
to tell (vt)	айтып берүү	ajtıp beryy

to find (vt)	табуу	tabuu
to get lost (lose one's way)	адашып кетүү	adaʃıp ketyy
map (e.g., subway ~)	схема	sχema
map (e.g., city ~)	план	plan

souvenir, gift	асембелек	asembelek
gift shop	асембелек дүкөнү	asembelek dykøny
to take pictures	сүрөткө тартуу	syrøtkø tartuu
to have one's picture taken	сүрөткө түшүү	syrøtkø tyʃyy

TRANSPORTATION

23. Airport

airport	аэропорт	aeroport
airplane	учак	utʃak
airline	авиакомпания	aviakompanija
air traffic controller	авиадиспетчер	aviadispettʃer
departure	учуп кетүү	utʃup ketyy
arrival	учуп келүү	utʃup kelyy
to arrive (by plane)	учуп келүү	utʃup kelyy
departure time	учуп кетүү убактысы	utʃup ketyy ubaktısı
arrival time	учуп келүү убактысы	utʃup kelyy ubaktısı
to be delayed	кармалуу	karmaluu
flight delay	учуп кетүүнүн кечигиши	utʃup ketyynyn ketʃigiʃi
information board	маалымат таблосу	maalımat tablosu
information	маалымат	maalımat
to announce (vt)	кулактандыруу	kulaktandıruu
flight (e.g., next ~)	рейс	rejs
customs	бажыкана	badʒıkana
customs officer	бажы кызматкери	badʒı kızmatkeri
customs declaration	бажы декларациясы	badʒı deklaratsijası
to fill out (vt)	толтуруу	tolturuu
to fill out the declaration	декларация толтуруу	deklaratsija tolturuu
passport control	паспорт текшерүү	pasport tekʃeryy
luggage	жүк	dʒyk
hand luggage	кол жүгү	kol dʒygy
luggage cart	араба	araba
landing	конуу	konuu
landing strip	конуу тилкеси	konuu tilkesi
to land (vi)	конуу	konuu
airstair (passenger stair)	трап	trap
check-in	катталуу	kattaluu
check-in counter	каттоо стойкасы	kattoo stojkası
to check-in (vi)	катталуу	kattaluu
boarding pass	отуруу үчүн талон	oturuu ytʃyn talon

departure gate	чыгуу	ʧɪguu
transit	транзит	tranzit
to wait (vt)	күтүү	kytyy
departure lounge	күтүү залы	kutyy zalı
to see off	узатуу	uzatuu
to say goodbye	коштошуу	koʃtoʃuu

24. Airplane

airplane	учак	uʧak
air ticket	авиабилет	aviabilet
airline	авиакомпания	aviakompanija
airport	аэропорт	aeroport
supersonic (adj)	сверхзвуковой	sverχzvukovoj

captain	кеме командири	keme komandiri
crew	экипаж	ekipadʒ
pilot	учкуч	uʧkuʧ
flight attendant (fem.)	стюардесса	stɥardessa
navigator	штурман	ʃturman

wings	канаттар	kanattar
tail	куйрук	kujruk
cockpit	кабина	kabina
engine	кыймылдаткыч	kıjmıldatkıʧ
undercarriage (landing gear)	шасси	ʃassi
turbine	турбина	turbina

propeller	пропеллер	propeller
black box	кара куту	kara kutu
yoke (control column)	штурвал	ʃturval
fuel	күйүүчү май	kyjyyʧy may

safety card	коопсуздук көрсөтмөсү	koopsuzduk kørsøtmøsy
oxygen mask	кислород чүмбөтү	kislorod ʧymbøty
uniform	бир беткей кийим	bir betkey kijim
life vest	куткаруучу күрмө	kutkaruuʧu kyrmø
parachute	парашют	paraʃut

takeoff	учуп көтөрүлүү	uʧup køtørylyy
to take off (vi)	учуп көтөрүлүү	uʧup køtørylyy
runway	учуп чыгуу тилкеси	uʧup ʧɪguu tilkesi

visibility	көрүнүш	kørynyʃ
flight (act of flying)	учуу	uʧuu
altitude	бийиктик	bijiktik
air pocket	аба чүңкуру	aba ʧyŋkuru
seat	орун	orun
headphones	кулакчын	kulakʧın

folding tray (tray table)	бүктөлмө стол	byktølmø stol
airplane window	иллюминатор	illuminator
aisle	өтмөк	øtmøk

25. Train

train	поезд	poezd
commuter train	электричка	elektritʃka
express train	бат жүрүүчү поезд	bat dʒyryytʃy poezd
diesel locomotive	тепловоз	teplovoz
steam locomotive	паровоз	parovoz

| passenger car | вагон | vagon |
| dining car | вагон-ресторан | vagon-restoran |

rails	рельсалар	relʲsalar
railroad	темир жолу	temir dʒolu
railway tie	шпала	ʃpala

platform (railway ~)	платформа	platforma
track (~ 1, 2, etc.)	жол	dʒol
semaphore	семафор	semafor
station	бекет	beket

engineer (train driver)	машинист	maʃinist
porter (of luggage)	жук ташуучу	dʒuk taʃuutʃu
car attendant	проводник	provodnik
passenger	жүргүнчү	dʒyrgyntʃy
conductor (ticket inspector)	текшерүүчү	tekʃeryytʃy

| corridor (in train) | коридор | koridor |
| emergency brake | стоп-кран | stop-kran |

compartment	купе	kupe
berth	текче	tektʃe
upper berth	үстүнкү текче	ystynky tektʃe
lower berth	ылдыйкы текче	ıldıjkı tektʃe
bed linen, bedding	жууркан-төшөк	dʒuurkan-tøʃøk

ticket	билет	bilet
schedule	ырааттама	ıraattama
information display	табло	tablo

to leave, to depart	жөнөө	dʒønøø
departure (of train)	жөнөө	dʒønøø
to arrive (ab. train)	келүү	kelyy
arrival	келүү	kelyy
to arrive by train	поезд менен келүү	poezd menen kelyy
to get on the train	поездге отуруу	poezdge oturuu

to get off the train	поездден түшүү	poezdden tyʃyy
train wreck	кыйроо	kıjroo
to derail (vi)	рельсадан чыгып кетүү	relʲsadan tʃıgıp ketyy

steam locomotive	паровоз	parovoz
stoker, fireman	от жагуучу	ot dʒaguutʃu
firebox	меш	meʃ
coal	көмүр	kømyr

26. Ship

| ship | кеме | keme |
| vessel | кеме | keme |

steamship	пароход	paroχod
riverboat	теплоход	teploχod
cruise ship	лайнер	lajner
cruiser	крейсер	krejser

yacht	яхта	jaχta
tugboat	буксир	buksir
barge	баржа	bardʒa
ferry	паром	parom

| sailing ship | парус | parus |
| brigantine | бригантина | brigantina |

| ice breaker | муз жаргыч кеме | muz dʒargıtʃ keme |
| submarine | суу астында жүрүүчү кеме | suu astında dʒyryytʃy keme |

boat (flat-bottomed ~)	кайык	kajık
dinghy	шлюпка	ʃlʉpka
lifeboat	куткаруу шлюпкасы	kutkaruu ʃlʉpkası
motorboat	катер	kater

captain	капитан	kapitan
seaman	матрос	matros
sailor	деңизчи	deŋiztʃi
crew	экипаж	ekipadʒ

boatswain	боцман	botsman
ship's boy	юнга	jʉnga
cook	кок	kok
ship's doctor	кеме доктуру	keme dokturu

deck	палуба	paluba
mast	мачта	matʃta
sail	парус	parus
hold	трюм	trʉm

bow (prow)	тумшук	tumʃuk
stern	кеменин арткы бөлүгү	kemenin artkı bølygy
oar	калак	kalak
screw propeller	винт	vint
cabin	каюта	kajʉta
wardroom	кают-компания	kajʉt-kompanija
engine room	машина бөлүгү	maʃina bølygy
bridge	капитан мостиги	kapitan mostigi
radio room	радиорубка	radiorubka
wave (radio)	толкун	tolkun
logbook	кеме журналы	keme dʒurnalı
spyglass	дүрбү	dyrby
bell	коңгуроо	koŋguroo
flag	байрак	bajrak
hawser (mooring ~)	аркан	arkan
knot (bowline, etc.)	түйүн	tyjyn
deckrails	туткуч	tutkuʧ
gangway	трап	trap
anchor	кеме казык	keme kazık
to weigh anchor	кеме казыкты көтөрүү	keme kazıktı køtøryy
to drop anchor	кеме казыкты таштоо	keme kazıktı taʃtoo
anchor chain	казык чынжыры	kazık ʧındʒırı
port (harbor)	порт	port
quay, wharf	причал	priʧal
to berth (moor)	келип токтоо	kelip toktoo
to cast off	жээктен алыстоо	dʒeekten alıstoo
trip, voyage	саякат	sajakat
cruise (sea trip)	деңиз саякаты	deŋiz sajakatı
course (route)	курс	kurs
route (itinerary)	каттам	kattam
fairway (safe water channel)	фарватер	farvater
shallows	тайыз жер	tajız dʒer
to run aground	тайыз жерге отуруу	tajız dʒerge oturuu
storm	бороон чапкын	boroon ʧapkın
signal	сигнал	signal
to sink (vi)	чөгүү	ʧøgyy
Man overboard!	Сууда адам бар!	suuda adam bar!
SOS (distress signal)	SOS	sos
ring buoy	куткаруучу тегерек	kutkaruuʧu tegerek

CITY

27. Urban transportation

bus	автобус	avtobus
streetcar	трамвай	tramvaj
trolley bus	троллейбус	trollejbus
route (of bus, etc.)	каттам	kattam
number (e.g., bus ~)	номер	nomer
to go by ...	... жүрүү	... dʒyryy
to get on (~ the bus)	... отуруу	... oturuu
to get off ...	... түшүп калуу	... tyʃyp kaluu
stop (e.g., bus ~)	аялдама	ajaldama
next stop	кийинки аялдама	kijinki ajaldama
terminus	акыркы аялдама	akırkı ajaldama
schedule	ырааттама	ıraattama
to wait (vt)	күтүү	kytyy
ticket	билет	bilet
fare	билеттин баасы	bilettin baası
cashier (ticket seller)	кассир	kassir
ticket inspection	текшерүү	tekʃeryy
ticket inspector	текшерүүчү	tekʃeryytʃy
to be late (for ...)	кечигүү	ketʃigyy
to miss (~ the train, etc.)	кечигип калуу	ketʃigip kaluu
to be in a hurry	шашуу	ʃaʃuu
taxi, cab	такси	taksi
taxi driver	такси айдоочу	taksi ajdootʃu
by taxi	таксиде	takside
taxi stand	такси токтоочу жай	taksi toktootʃu dʒaj
to call a taxi	такси чакыруу	taksi tʃakıruu
to take a taxi	такси кармоо	taksi karmoo
traffic	көчө кыймылы	køtʃø kıjmılı
traffic jam	тыгын	tıgın
rush hour	кызуу маал	kızuu maal
to park (vi)	токтотуу	toktotuu
to park (vt)	машинаны жайлаштыруу	maʃinanı dʒajlaʃtıruu
parking lot	унаа токтоочу жай	unaa toktootʃu dʒaj
subway	метро	metro

station	бекет	beket
to take the subway	метродо жүрүү	metrodo dʒyryy
train	поезд	poezd
train station	вокзал	vokzal

28. City. Life in the city

city, town	шаар	ʃaar
capital city	борбор	borbor
village	кыштак	kɪʃtak

city map	шаардын планы	ʃaardın planı
downtown	шаардын борбору	ʃaardın borboru
suburb	шаардын чет жакасы	ʃaardın tʃet dʒakası
suburban (adj)	шаардын чет жакасындагы	ʃaardın tʃet dʒakasındagı

outskirts	чет-жака	tʃet-dʒaka
environs (suburbs)	чет-жака	tʃet-dʒaka
city block	квартал	kvartal
residential block (area)	турак-жай кварталы	turak-dʒaj kvartalı

traffic	көчө кыймылы	køtʃø kıjmılı
traffic lights	светофор	svetofor
public transportation	шаар транспорту	ʃaar transportu
intersection	кесилиш	kesiliʃ

crosswalk	жөө жүрүүчүлөр жолу	dʒøø dʒyryytʃylør dʒolu
pedestrian underpass	жер астындагы жол	dʒer astındagı dʒol
to cross (~ the street)	жолду өтүү	dʒoldu øtyy
pedestrian	жөө жүрүүчү	dʒøø dʒyryytʃy
sidewalk	жанжол	dʒandʒol

bridge	көпүрө	køpyrø
embankment (river walk)	жээк жол	dʒeek dʒol
fountain	фонтан	fontan

allée (garden walkway)	аллея	alleja
park	сейил багы	sejil bagı
boulevard	бульвар	bulʲvar
square	аянт	ajant
avenue (wide street)	проспект	prospekt
street	көчө	køtʃø
side street	чолок көчө	tʃolok køtʃø
dead end	туюк көчө	tujuk køtʃø

house	үй	yj
building	имарат	imarat
skyscraper	көк тиреген көп кабаттуу үй	køk tiregen køp kabattuu yj

facade	үйдүн алды	yjdyn aldı
roof	чатыр	tʃatır
window	терезе	tereze
arch	түркүк	tyrkyk
column	мамы	mamı
corner	бурч	burtʃ

store window	көрсөтмө айнек үкөк	kørsøtmø ajnek ykøk
signboard (store sign, etc.)	көрнөк	kørnøk
poster (e.g., playbill)	афиша	afiʃa
advertising poster	көрнөк-жарнак	kørnøk-dʒarnak
billboard	жарнамалык такта	dʒarnamalık takta

garbage, trash	таштанды	taʃtandı
trash can (public ~)	таштанды челек	taʃtandı tʃelek
to litter (vi)	таштоо	taʃtoo
garbage dump	таштанды үйүлгөн жер	taʃtandı yjylgøn dʒer

phone booth	телефон будкасы	telefon budkası
lamppost	чырак мамы	tʃırak mamı
bench (park ~)	отургуч	oturgutʃ

police officer	полиция кызматкери	politsija kızmatkeri
police	полиция	politsija
beggar	кайырчы	kajırtʃı
homeless (n)	селсаяк	selsajak

29. Urban institutions

store	дүкөн	dykøn
drugstore, pharmacy	дарыкана	darıkana
eyeglass store	оптика	optika
shopping mall	соода борбору	sooda borboru
supermarket	супермаркет	supermarket

bakery	нан дүкөнү	nan dykøny
baker	навайчы	navajtʃı
pastry shop	кондитердик дүкөн	konditerdik dykøn
grocery store	азык-түлүк	azık-tylyk
butcher shop	эт дүкөнү	et dykøny

| produce store | жашылча дүкөнү | dʒaʃiltʃa dykøny |
| market | базар | bazar |

coffee house	кофекана	kofekana
restaurant	ресторан	restoran
pub, bar	сыракана	sırakana
pizzeria	пиццерия	pitserija
hair salon	чач тарач	tʃatʃ taratʃ
post office	почта	potʃta

dry cleaners	химиялык тазалоо	χimijalık tazaloo
photo studio	фотоателье	fotoatelje
shoe store	бут кийим дүкөнү	but kijim dykøny
bookstore	китеп дүкөнү	kitep dykøny
sporting goods store	спорт буюмдар дүкөнү	sport bujumdar dykøny
clothes repair shop	кийим ондоочу жай	kijim ondootʃu dʒaj
formal wear rental	кийимди ижарага берүү	kijimdi idʒaraga beryy
video rental store	тасмаларды ижарага берүү	tasmalardı idʒaraga beryy
circus	цирк	tsırk
zoo	зоопарк	zoopark
movie theater	кинотеатр	kinoteatr
museum	музей	muzej
library	китепкана	kitepkana
theater	театр	teatr
opera (opera house)	опера	opera
nightclub	түнкү клуб	tynky klub
casino	казино	kazino
mosque	мечит	metʃit
synagogue	синагога	sinagoga
cathedral	чоң чиркөө	tʃoŋ tʃirkøø
temple	ибадаткана	ibadatkana
church	чиркөө	tʃirkøø
college	коллеж	kolledʒ
university	университет	universitet
school	мектеп	mektep
prefecture	префектура	prefektura
city hall	мэрия	merija
hotel	мейманкана	mejmankana
bank	банк	bank
embassy	элчилик	eltʃilik
travel agency	турагенттиги	turagenttigi
information office	маалымат бюросу	maalımat burosu
currency exchange	алмаштыруу пункту	almaʃtıruu punktu
subway	метро	metro
hospital	оорукана	oorukana
gas station	май куюучу станция	maj kujuutʃu stantsija
parking lot	унаа токтоочу жай	unaa toktootʃu dʒaj

30. Signs

signboard (store sign, etc.)	көрнөк	kørnøk
notice (door sign, etc.)	жазуу	dʒazuu
poster	көрнөк	kørnøk
direction sign	көрсөткүч	kørsøtkytʃ
arrow (sign)	жебе	dʒebe
caution	экертме	ekertme
warning sign	эскертүү белгиси	eskertyy belgisi
to warn (vt)	эскертүү	eskertyy
rest day (weekly ~)	дем алыш күн	dem alıʃ kyn
timetable (schedule)	ырааттама	ıraattama
opening hours	иш сааттары	iʃ saattarı
WELCOME!	КОШ КЕЛИҢИЗДЕР!	koʃ keliŋizder!
ENTRANCE	КИРҮҮ	kiryy
EXIT	ЧЫГУУ	tʃıguu
PUSH	ӨЗҮҢҮЗДӨН ТҮРТҮҢҮЗ	øzyŋyzdøn tyrtyŋyz
PULL	ӨЗҮҢҮЗГӨ ТАРТЫҢЫЗ	øzyŋyzgø tartıŋız
OPEN	АЧЫК	atʃık
CLOSED	ЖАБЫК	dʒabık
WOMEN	АЙЫМДАР ҮЧҮН	ajımdar ytʃyn
MEN	ЭРКЕКТЕР ҮЧҮН	erkekter ytʃyn
DISCOUNTS	АРЗАНДАТУУЛАР	arzandatuular
SALE	САТЫП ТҮГӨТҮҮ	satıp tygøtyy
NEW!	СААМАЛЫК!	saamalık!
FREE	БЕКЕР	beker
ATTENTION!	КӨҢҮЛ БУРУҢУЗ!	køŋyl buruŋuz!
NO VACANCIES	ОРУН ЖОК	orun dʒok
RESERVED	КАМДЫК	kamdık
	БУЙРУТМАЛАГАН	bujrutmalagan
ADMINISTRATION	АДМИНИСТРАЦИЯ	administratsija
STAFF ONLY	ЖААМАТ ҮЧҮН ГАНА	dʒaamat ytʃyn gana
BEWARE OF THE DOG!	КАБАНААК ИТ	kabanaak it
NO SMOKING	ТАМЕКИ ЧЕГҮҮГӨ БОЛБОЙТ!	tameki tʃegyygø bolbojt!
DO NOT TOUCH!	КОЛУҢАР МЕНЕН КАРМАБАГЫЛА!	koluŋar menen karmabagıla!
DANGEROUS	КООПТУУ	kooptuu
DANGER	КОРКУНУЧ	korkunutʃ
HIGH VOLTAGE	ЖОГОРКУ ЧЫҢАЛУУ	dʒogorku tʃıŋaluu
NO SWIMMING!	СУУГА ТҮШҮҮГӨ БОЛБОЙТ	suuga tyʃyygø bolbojt

OUT OF ORDER	ИШТЕБЕЙТ	iʃtebejt
FLAMMABLE	ӨРТ ЧЫГУУ КОРКУНУЧУ	ørt tʃiguu korkunutʃu
FORBIDDEN	ТЫЮУ САЛЫНГАН	tijuu salıngan
NO TRESPASSING!	ӨТҮҮГӨ БОЛБОЙТ	øtyygø bolbojt
WET PAINT	СЫРДАЛГАН	sırdalgan

31. Shopping

to buy (purchase)	сатып алуу	satıp aluu
purchase	сатып алуу	satıp aluu
to go shopping	сатып алууга чыгуу	satıp aluuga tʃiguu
shopping	базарчылоо	bazartʃiloo

| to be open (ab. store) | иштөө | iʃtøø |
| to be closed | жабылуу | dʒabıluu |

footwear, shoes	бут кийим	but kijim
clothes, clothing	кийим-кече	kijim-ketʃe
cosmetics	упа-эндик	upa-endik
food products	азык-түлүк	azık-tylyk
gift, present	белек	belek

| salesman | сатуучу | satuutʃu |
| saleswoman | сатуучу кыз | satuutʃu kız |

check out, cash desk	касса	kassa
mirror	күзгү	kyzgy
counter (store ~)	прилавок	prilavok
fitting room	кийим ченөөчү бөлмө	kijim tʃenøøtʃy bølmø

to try on	кийим ченөө	kijim tʃenøø
to fit (ab. dress, etc.)	ылайык келүү	ılajık kelyy
to like (I like …)	жактыруу	dʒaktıruu

price	баа	baa
price tag	баа	baa
to cost (vt)	туруу	turuu
How much?	Канча?	kantʃa?
discount	арзандатуу	arzandatuu

inexpensive (adj)	кымбат эмес	kımbat emes
cheap (adj)	арзан	arzan
expensive (adj)	кымбат	kımbat
It's expensive	Бул кымбат	bul kımbat

rental (n)	ижара	idʒara
to rent (~ a tuxedo)	ижарага алуу	idʒaraga aluu
credit (trade credit)	насыя	nasıja
on credit (adv)	насыяга алуу	nasıjaga aluu

CLOTHING & ACCESSORIES

32. Outerwear. Coats

clothes	кийим	kijim
outerwear	үстүңкү кийим	ystyŋky kijim
winter clothing	кышкы кийим	kıʃkı kijim
coat (overcoat)	пальто	palʲto
fur coat	тон	ton
fur jacket	чолок тон	tʃolok ton
down coat	мамык олпок	mamık olpok
jacket (e.g., leather ~)	күрмө	kyrmø
raincoat (trenchcoat, etc.)	плащ	plaʃtʃ
waterproof (adj)	суу өткүс	suu øtkys

33. Men's & women's clothing

shirt (button shirt)	көйнөк	køjnøk
pants	шым	ʃim
jeans	джинсы	dʒinsı
suit jacket	бешмант	beʃmant
suit	костюм	kostʉm
dress (frock)	көйнөк	køjnøk
skirt	юбка	jʉbka
blouse	блузка	bluzka
knitted jacket (cardigan, etc.)	кофта	kofta
jacket (of woman's suit)	кыска бешмант	kıska beʃmant
T-shirt	футболка	futbolka
shorts (short trousers)	чолок шым	tʃolok ʃim
tracksuit	спорт кийими	sport kijimi
bathrobe	халат	χalat
pajamas	пижама	pidʒama
sweater	свитер	sviter
pullover	пуловер	pulover
vest	жилет	dʒilet
tailcoat	фрак	frak
tuxedo	смокинг	smoking

uniform	форма	forma
workwear	жумуш кийим	dʒumuʃ kijim
overalls	комбинезон	kombinezon
coat (e.g., doctor's smock)	халат	χalat

34. Clothing. Underwear

underwear	ич кийим	itʃ kijim
boxers, briefs	эркектер чолок	erkekter ʧolok
	дамбалы	dambalı
panties	аялдар трусиги	ajaldar trusigi
undershirt (A-shirt)	майка	majka
socks	байпак	bajpak
nightdress	жатаарда кийүүчү	dʒataarda kijyyʧy
	көйнөк	køjnøk
bra	бюстгальтер	buѕtgalʲter
knee highs	гольфы	golʲfı
(knee-high socks)		
pantyhose	колготки	kolgotki
stockings (thigh highs)	байпак	bajpak
bathing suit	купальник	kupalʲnik

35. Headwear

hat	топу	topu
fedora	шляпа	ʃlʲapa
baseball cap	бейсболка	bejsbolka
flatcap	кепка	kepka
beret	берет	beret
hood	капюшон	kapʉʃon
panama hat	панамка	panamka
knit cap (knitted hat)	токулган шапка	tokulgan ʃapka
headscarf	жоолук	dʒooluk
women's hat	шляпа	ʃlʲapa
hard hat	каска	kaska
garrison cap	пилотка	pilotka
helmet	шлем	ʃlem
derby	котелок	kotelok
top hat	цилиндр	tsılindr

36. Footwear

footwear	бут кийим	but kijim
shoes (men's shoes)	ботинка	botinka
shoes (women's shoes)	туфли	tufli
boots (e.g., cowboy ~)	өтүк	øtyk
slippers	тапочка	tapotʃka

tennis shoes (e.g., Nike ~)	кроссовка	krossovka
sneakers (e.g., Converse ~)	кеды	kedı
sandals	сандалии	sandalii

cobbler (shoe repairer)	өтүкчү	øtyktʃy
heel	така	taka
pair (of shoes)	түгөй	tygøj

shoestring	боо	boo
to lace (vt)	боолоо	booloo
shoehorn	кашык	kaʃık
shoe polish	өтүк май	øtyk maj

37. Personal accessories

gloves	колкап	kolkap
mittens	мээлей	meelej
scarf (muffler)	моюн орогуч	mojun orogutʃ

glasses (eyeglasses)	көз айнек	køz ajnek
frame (eyeglass ~)	алкак	alkak
umbrella	чатырча	tʃatırtʃa
walking stick	аса таяк	asa tajak
hairbrush	тарак	tarak
fan	желпингич	dʒelpingitʃ
tie (necktie)	галстук	galstuk
bow tie	галстук-бабочка	galstuk-babotʃka
suspenders	шым тарткыч	ʃım tartkıtʃ
handkerchief	бетаарчы	betaartʃı

comb	тарак	tarak
barrette	чачсайгы	tʃatʃsajgı
hairpin	шпилька	ʃpilʲka
buckle	таралга	taralga

belt	кайыш кур	kajıʃ kur
shoulder strap	илгич	ilgitʃ
bag (handbag)	колбаштык	kolbaʃtık
purse	кичине колбаштык	kitʃine kolbaʃtık
backpack	жонбаштык	dʒonbaʃtık

38. Clothing. Miscellaneous

fashion	мода	moda
in vogue (adj)	саркеч	sarketʃ
fashion designer	модельер	modeljer
collar	жака	ʤaka
pocket	чөнтөк	tʃøntøk
pocket (as adj)	чөнтөк	tʃøntøk
sleeve	жең	ʤeŋ
hanging loop	илгич	ilgitʃ
fly (on trousers)	ширинка	ʃirinka
zipper (fastener)	молния	molnija
fastener	топчулук	toptʃuluk
button	топчу	toptʃu
buttonhole	илмек	ilmek
to come off (ab. button)	үзүлүү	yzylyy
to sew (vi, vt)	тигүү	tigyy
to embroider (vi, vt)	сайма саюу	sajma sajɯu
embroidery	сайма	sajma
sewing needle	ийне	ijne
thread	жип	ʤip
seam	тигиш	tigiʃ
to get dirty (vi)	булгап алуу	bulgap aluu
stain (mark, spot)	так	tak
to crease, crumple (vi)	бырышып калуу	bɯrɯʃɯp kaluu
to tear, to rip (vt)	айрылуу	ajrɯluu
clothes moth	күбө	kybø

39. Personal care. Cosmetics

toothpaste	тиш пастасы	tiʃ pastasɯ
toothbrush	тиш щёткасы	tiʃ ʃtʃotkasɯ
to brush one's teeth	тиш жуу	tiʃ ʤuu
razor	устара	ustara
shaving cream	кырынуу үчүн көбүк	kɯrɯnuu ytʃyn købyk
to shave (vi)	кырынуу	kɯrɯnuu
soap	самын	samɯn
shampoo	шампунь	ʃampunʲ
scissors	кайчы	kajtʃɯ
nail file	тырмак өгөө	tɯrmak øgøø
nail clippers	тырмак кычкачы	tɯrmak kɯtʃkatʃɯ
tweezers	искек	iskek

cosmetics	упа-эндик	upa-endik
face mask	маска	maska
manicure	маникюр	manikʉr
to have a manicure	маникюр жасоо	manikdʒʉr dʒasoo
pedicure	педикюр	pedikʉr

make-up bag	косметичка	kosmetitʃka
face powder	упа	upa
powder compact	упа кутусу	upa kutusu
blusher	эндик	endik

perfume (bottled)	атыр	atır
toilet water (lotion)	туалет атыр суусу	tualet atır suusu
lotion	лосьон	losʲon
cologne	одеколон	odekolon

eyeshadow	көз боёгу	køz bojogu
eyeliner	көз карандашы	køz karandaʃı
mascara	кирпик үчүн боек	kirpik ytʃyn boek

lipstick	эрин помадасы	erin pomadası
nail polish, enamel	тырмак үчүн лак	tırmak ytʃyn lak
hair spray	чач үчүн лак	tʃatʃ ytʃyn lak
deodorant	дезодорант	dezodorant

cream	крем	krem
face cream	бетмай	betmaj
hand cream	кол үчүн май	kol ytʃyn maj
anti-wrinkle cream	бырыштарга каршы бет май	bırıʃtarga karʃı bet maj
day cream	күндүзгү бет май	kyndyzgy bet maj
night cream	түнкү бет май	tynky bet maj
day (as adj)	күндүзгү	kyndyzgy
night (as adj)	түнкү	tynky

tampon	тампон	tampon
toilet paper (toilet roll)	даарат кагазы	daarat kagazı
hair dryer	фен	fen

40. Watches. Clocks

watch (wristwatch)	кол саат	kol saat
dial	циферблат	tsıferblat
hand (of clock, watch)	жебе	dʒebe
metal watch band	браслет	braslet
watch strap	кайыш кур	kajıʃ kur

battery	батарейка	batarejka
to be dead (battery)	зарядканын түгөнүүсү	zarʲadkanın tygønyysy
to change a battery	батарейка алмаштыруу	batarejka almaʃtıruu

| to run fast | алдыга кетүү | aldıga ketyy |
| to run slow | калуу | kaluu |

wall clock	дубалга тагуучу саат	dubalga taguutʃu saat
hourglass	кум саат	kum saat
sundial	күн саат	kyn saat
alarm clock	ойготкуч саат	ojgotkutʃ saat
watchmaker	саат устасы	saat ustası
to repair (vt)	оңдоо	oŋdoo

EVERYDAY EXPERIENCE

41. Money

money	акча	aktʃa
currency exchange	алмаштыруу	almaʃtıruu
exchange rate	курс	kurs
ATM	банкомат	bankomat
coin	тыйын	tıjın
dollar	доллар	dollar
euro	евро	evro
lira	италиялык лира	italijalık lira
Deutschmark	немис маркасы	nemis markası
franc	франк	frank
pound sterling	фунт стерлинг	funt sterling
yen	йена	jena
debt	карыз	karız
debtor	карыздар	karızdar
to lend (money)	карызга берүү	karızga beryy
to borrow (vi, vt)	карызга алуу	karızga aluu
bank	банк	bank
account	эсеп	esep
to deposit (vt)	салуу	saluu
to deposit into the account	эсепке акча салуу	esepke aktʃa saluu
to withdraw (vt)	эсептен акча чыгаруу	esepten aktʃa tʃıgaruu
credit card	насыя картасы	nasıja kartası
cash	накталай акча	naktalaj aktʃa
check	чек	tʃek
to write a check	чек жазып берүү	tʃek dʒazıp beryy
checkbook	чек китепчеси	tʃek kiteptʃesi
wallet	намыян	namıjan
change purse	капчык	kaptʃık
safe	сейф	sejf
heir	мураскер	murasker
inheritance	мурас	muras
fortune (wealth)	мүлк	mylk
lease	ижара	idʒara
rent (money)	батир акысы	batir akısı

to rent (sth from sb)	батирге алуу	batirge aluu
price	баа	baa
cost	баа	baa
sum	сумма	summa
to spend (vt)	коротуу	korotuu
expenses	чыгым	tʃɪgɪm
to economize (vi, vt)	үнөмдөө	ynømdøø
economical	сарамжал	saramdʒal
to pay (vi, vt)	төлөө	tøløø
payment	акы төлөө	akɪ tøløø
change (give the ~)	кайтарылган майда акча	kajtarɪlgan majda aktʃa
tax	салык	salɪk
fine	айып	ajɪp
to fine (vt)	айып пул салуу	ajɪp pul saluu

42. Post. Postal service

post office	почта	potʃta
mail (letters, etc.)	почта	potʃta
mailman	кат ташуучу	kat taʃuutʃu
opening hours	иш сааттары	iʃ saattarɪ
letter	кат	kat
registered letter	тапшырык кат	tapʃɪrɪk kat
postcard	открытка	otkrɪtka
telegram	телеграмма	telegramma
package (parcel)	посылка	posɪlka
money transfer	акча которуу	aktʃa kotoruu
to receive (vt)	алуу	aluu
to send (vt)	жөнөтүү	dʒønøtyy
sending	жөнөтүү	dʒønøtyy
address	дарек	darek
ZIP code	индекс	indeks
sender	жөнөтүүчү	dʒønøtyytʃy
receiver	алуучу	aluutʃu
name (first name)	аты	atɪ
surname (last name)	фамилиясы	familijasɪ
postage rate	тариф	tarif
standard (adj)	жөнөкөй	dʒønøkøj
economical (adj)	үнөмдүү	ynømdyy
weight	салмак	salmak
to weigh (~ letters)	таразалоо	tarazaloo

envelope	конверт	konvert
postage stamp	марка	marka
to stamp an envelope	марка жабыштыруу	marka dʒabıʃtıruu

43. Banking

| bank | банк | bank |
| branch (of bank, etc.) | бөлүм | bølym |

| bank clerk, consultant | кеңешчи | keŋeʃʧi |
| manager (director) | башкарууучу | baʃkaruuʧu |

bank account	эсеп	esep
account number	эсеп номери	esep nomeri
checking account	учурдагы эсеп	uʧurdagı esep
savings account	топтолмо эсеп	toptolmo esep

to open an account	эсеп ачуу	esep aʧuu
to close the account	эсеп жабуу	esep dʒabuu
to deposit into the account	эсепке акча салуу	esepke akʧa saluu
to withdraw (vt)	эсептен акча чыгаруу	esepten akʧa ʧıgaruu

| deposit | аманат | amanat |
| to make a deposit | аманат кылуу | amanat kıluu |

| wire transfer | акча которуу | akʧa kotoruu |
| to wire, to transfer | акча которуу | akʧa kotoruu |

| sum | сумма | summa |
| How much? | Канча? | kanʧa? |

| signature | кол тамга | kol tamga |
| to sign (vt) | кол коюу | kol kojɥu |

| credit card | насыя картасы | nasıja kartası |
| code (PIN code) | код | kod |

| credit card number | насыя картанын номери | nasıja kartanın nomeri |
| ATM | банкомат | bankomat |

check	чек	ʧek
to write a check	чек жазып берүү	ʧek dʒazıp beryy
checkbook	чек китепчеси	ʧek kitepʧesi

loan (bank ~)	насыя	nasıja
to apply for a loan	насыя үчүн кайрылуу	nasıja yʧyn kajrıluu
to get a loan	насыя алуу	nasıja aluu
to give a loan	насыя берүү	nasıja beryy
guarantee	кепилдик	kepildik

44. Telephone. Phone conversation

telephone	телефон	telefon
cell phone	мобилдик	mobildik
answering machine	автоматтык жооп берүүчү	avtomattık dʒoop beryytʃy
to call (by phone)	чалуу	tʃaluu
phone call	чакыруу	tʃakıruu
to dial a number	номер терүү	nomer teryy
Hello!	Алло!	allo!
to ask (vt)	суроо	suroo
to answer (vi, vt)	жооп берүү	dʒoop beryy
to hear (vt)	угуу	uguu
well (adv)	жакшы	dʒakʃı
not well (adv)	жаман	dʒaman
noises (interference)	ызы-чуу	ızı-tʃuu
receiver	трубка	trubka
to pick up (~ the phone)	трубканы алуу	trubkanı aluu
to hang up (~ the phone)	трубканы коюу	trubkanı kojʉu
busy (engaged)	бош эмес	boʃ emes
to ring (ab. phone)	шыңгыроо	ʃıŋgıroo
telephone book	телефондук китепче	telefonduk kiteptʃe
local (adj)	жергиликтүү	dʒergiliktyy
local call	жергиликтүү чакыруу	dʒergiliktyy tʃakıruu
long distance (~ call)	шаар аралык	ʃaar aralık
long-distance call	шаар аралык чакыруу	ʃaar aralık tʃakıruu
international (adj)	эл аралык	el aralık
international call	эл аралык чакыруу	el aralık tʃakıruu

45. Cell phone

cell phone	мобилдик	mobildik
display	дисплей	displej
button	баскыч	baskıtʃ
SIM card	SIM-карта	sim-karta
battery	батарея	batareja
to be dead (battery)	зарядканын түгөнүүсү	zarʲadkanın tygønyysy
charger	заряддоочу шайман	zarʲaddootʃu ʃajman
menu	меню	menʉ
settings	орнотуулар	ornotuular
tune (melody)	обон	obon

to select (vt)	тандоо	tandoo
calculator	калькулятор	kalʲkulʲator
voice mail	автоматтык жооп бергич	avtomattık dʒoop bergitʃ
alarm clock	ойготкуч	ojgotkutʃ
contacts	байланыштар	bajlanıʃtar
SMS (text message)	SMS-кабар	esemes-kabar
subscriber	абонент	abonent

46. Stationery

ballpoint pen	калем сап	kalem sap
fountain pen	калем уч	kalem utʃ
pencil	карандаш	karandaʃ
highlighter	маркер	marker
felt-tip pen	фломастер	flomaster
notepad	дептерче	deptertʃe
agenda (diary)	күндөлүк	kyndølyk
ruler	сызгыч	sızgıtʃ
calculator	калькулятор	kalʲkulʲator
eraser	өчүргүч	øtʃyrgytʃ
thumbtack	кнопка	knopka
paper clip	кыскыч	kıskıtʃ
glue	желим	dʒelim
stapler	степлер	stepler
hole punch	тешкич	teʃkitʃ
pencil sharpener	учтагыч	utʃtagıtʃ

47. Foreign languages

language	тил	til
foreign (adj)	чет	tʃet
foreign language	чет тил	tʃet til
to study (vt)	окуу	okuu
to learn (language, etc.)	үйрөнүү	yjrønyy
to read (vi, vt)	окуу	okuu
to speak (vi, vt)	сүйлөө	syjløø
to understand (vt)	түшүнүү	tyʃynyy
to write (vt)	жазуу	dʒazuu
fast (adv)	тез	tez
slowly (adv)	жай	dʒaj

fluently (adv)	эркин	erkin
rules	эрежелер	ereӡeler
grammar	грамматика	grammatika
vocabulary	лексика	leksika
phonetics	фонетика	fonetika
textbook	китеп	kitep
dictionary	сөздүк	søzdyk
teach-yourself book	өзү үйрөткүч	øzy yjrøtkytʃ
phrasebook	тилачар	tilatʃar
cassette, tape	кассета	kasseta
videotape	видеокассета	videokasseta
CD, compact disc	CD, компакт-диск	sidi, kompakt-disk
DVD	DVD-диск	dividi-disk
alphabet	алфавит	alfavit
to spell (vt)	эжелеп айтуу	eӡelep ajtuu
pronunciation	айтылышы	ajtılıʃı
accent	акцент	aktsent
with an accent	акцент менен	aktsent menen
without an accent	акцентсиз	aktsentsiz
word	сөз	søz
meaning	маани	maani
course (e.g., a French ~)	курстар	kurstar
to sign up	курска жазылуу	kurska ӡazıluu
teacher	окутуучу	okutuutʃu
translation (process)	которуу	kotoruu
translation (text, etc.)	котормо	kotormo
translator	котормочу	kotormotʃu
interpreter	оозеки котормочу	oozeki kotormotʃu
polyglot	полиглот	poliglot
memory	эс тутум	es tutum

MEALS. RESTAURANT

48. Table setting

spoon	кашык	kaʃik
knife	бычак	bɪtʃak
fork	вилка	vilka
cup (e.g., coffee ~)	чөйчөк	tʃøjtʃøk
plate (dinner ~)	табак	tabak
saucer	табак	tabak
napkin (on table)	майлык	majlık
toothpick	тиш чукугуч	tiʃ tʃukugutʃ

49. Restaurant

restaurant	ресторан	restoran
coffee house	кофекана	kofekana
pub, bar	бар	bar
tearoom	чай салону	tʃaj salonu
waiter	официант	ofitsiant
waitress	официант кыз	ofitsiant kız
bartender	бармен	barmen
menu	меню	menʉ
wine list	шарап картасы	ʃarap kartası
to book a table	столду камдык	stoldu kamdık
	буйрутмалоо	bujrutmaloo
course, dish	тамак	tamak
to order (meal)	буйрутма кылуу	bujrutma kıluu
to make an order	буйрутма берүү	bujrutma beryy
aperitif	аперитив	aperitiv
appetizer	ысылык	ısılık
dessert	десерт	desert
check	эсеп	esep
to pay the check	эсеп төлөө	esep tøløø
to give change	майда акчаны кайтаруу	majda aktʃanı kajtaruu
tip	чайпул	tʃajpul

50. Meals

food	тамак	tamak
to eat (vi, vt)	тамактануу	tamaktanuu
breakfast	таңкы тамак	taŋkı tamak
to have breakfast	эртең менен тамактануу	erteŋ menen tamaktanuu
lunch	түшкү тамак	tyʃky tamak
to have lunch	түштөнүү	tyʃtønyy
dinner	кечки тамак	ketʃki tamak
to have dinner	кечки тамакты ичүү	ketʃki tamaktı itʃyy
appetite	табит	tabit
Enjoy your meal!	Тамагыңыз таттуу болсун!	tamagıŋız tattuu bolsun!
to open (~ a bottle)	ачуу	atʃuu
to spill (liquid)	төгүп алуу	tøgyp aluu
to spill out (vi)	төгүлүү	tøgylyy
to boil (vi)	кайноо	kajnoo
to boil (vt)	кайнатуу	kajnatuu
boiled (~ water)	кайнатылган	kajnatılgan
to chill, cool down (vt)	суутуу	suutuu
to chill (vi)	сууп туруу	suup turuu
taste, flavor	даам	daam
aftertaste	даамдануу	daamdanuu
to slim down (lose weight)	арыктоо	arıktoo
diet	мүнөз тамак	mynøz tamak
vitamin	витамин	vitamin
calorie	калория	kalorija
vegetarian (n)	эттен чанган	etten tʃangan
vegetarian (adj)	этсиз даярдалган	etsiz dajardalgan
fats (nutrient)	майлар	majlar
proteins	белоктор	beloktor
carbohydrates	көмүрсуулар	kømyrsuular
slice (of lemon, ham)	кесим	kesim
piece (of cake, pie)	бөлүк	bølyk
crumb (of bread, cake, etc.)	күкүм	kykym

51. Cooked dishes

course, dish	тамак	tamak
cuisine	даам	daam

| recipe | тамак жасоо ыкмасы | tamak dʒasoo ıkması |
| portion | порция | portsija |

| salad | салат | salat |
| soup | сорпо | sorpo |

clear soup (broth)	ынак сорпо	ınak sorpo
sandwich (bread)	бутерброд	buterbrod
fried eggs	куурулган жумуртка	kuurulgan dʒumurtka
hamburger (beefburger)	гамбургер	gamburger
beefsteak	бифштекс	bifʃteks

side dish	гарнир	garnir
spaghetti	спагетти	spagetti
mashed potatoes	эзилген картошка	ezilgen kartoʃka
pizza	пицца	pitsa
porridge (oatmeal, etc.)	ботко	botko
omelet	омлет	omlet

boiled (e.g., ~ beef)	сууга бышырылган	suuga bıʃırılgan
smoked (adj)	ышталган	ıʃtalgan
fried (adj)	куурулган	kuurulgan
dried (adj)	кургатылган	kurgatılgan
frozen (adj)	тоңдурулган	toŋdurulgan
pickled (adj)	маринаддагы	marinaddagı

sweet (sugary)	таттуу	tattuu
salty (adj)	туздуу	tuzduu
cold (adj)	муздак	muzdak
hot (adj)	ысык	ısık
bitter (adj)	ачуу	atʃuu
tasty (adj)	даамдуу	daamduu

to cook in boiling water	кайнатуу	kajnatuu
to cook (dinner)	тамак бышыруу	tamak bıʃıruu
to fry (vt)	кууруу	kuuruu
to heat up (food)	жылытуу	dʒılıtuu

to salt (vt)	туздоо	tuzdoo
to pepper (vt)	калемпир кошуу	kalempir koʃuu
to grate (vt)	сүргүлөө	syrgyløø
peel (n)	сырты	sırtı
to peel (vt)	тазалоо	tazaloo

52. Food

meat	эт	et
chicken	тоок	took
Rock Cornish hen (poussin)	балапан	balapan

duck	өрдөк	ørdøk
goose	каз	kaz
game	илбээсин	ilbeesin
turkey	күрп	kyrp
pork	чочко эти	tʃotʃko eti
veal	торпок эти	torpok eti
lamb	кой эти	koj eti
beef	уй эти	uj eti
rabbit	коен	koen
sausage (bologna, etc.)	колбаса	kolbasa
vienna sausage (frankfurter)	сосиска	sosiska
bacon	бекон	bekon
ham	ветчина	vettʃina
gammon	сан эт	san et
pâté	паштет	paʃtet
liver	боор	boor
hamburger (ground beef)	фарш	farʃ
tongue	тил	til
egg	жумуртка	dʒumurtka
eggs	жумурткалар	dʒumurtkalar
egg white	жумуртканын агы	dʒumurtkanın agı
egg yolk	жумуртканын сарысы	dʒumurtkanın sarısı
fish	балык	balık
seafood	деңиз азыктары	deŋiz azıktarı
crustaceans	рак сыяктуулар	rak sıjaktuular
caviar	урук	uruk
crab	краб	krab
shrimp	креветка	krevetka
oyster	устрица	ustritsa
spiny lobster	лангуст	langust
octopus	сегиз бут	segiz but
squid	кальмар	kalʲmar
sturgeon	осетрина	osetrina
salmon	лосось	lososʲ
halibut	палтус	paltus
cod	треска	treska
mackerel	скумбрия	skumbrija
tuna	тунец	tunets
eel	угорь	ugorʲ
trout	форель	forelʲ
sardine	сардина	sardina
pike	чортон	tʃorton

herring	сельдь	selʲdʲ
bread	нан	nan
cheese	сыр	sır
sugar	кум шекер	kum-ʃeker
salt	туз	tuz

rice	күрүч	kyryʧ
pasta (macaroni)	макарон	makaron
noodles	кесме	kesme

butter	ак май	ak maj
vegetable oil	өсүмдүк майы	øsymdyk majı
sunflower oil	күн карама майы	kyn karama majı
margarine	маргарин	margarin

| olives | зайтун | zajtun |
| olive oil | зайтун майы | zajtun majı |

milk	сүт	syt
condensed milk	коютулган сүт	kojʉtulgan syt
yogurt	йогурт	jogurt
sour cream	сметана	smetana
cream (of milk)	каймак	kajmak

| mayonnaise | майонез | majonez |
| buttercream | крем | krem |

groats (barley ~, etc.)	акшак	akʃak
flour	ун	un
canned food	консерва	konserva

cornflakes	жарылган жүгөрү	ʤarılgan ʤygøry
honey	бал	bal
jam	джем, конфитюр	ʤem, konfitʉr
chewing gum	сагыз	sagız

53. Drinks

water	суу	suu
drinking water	ичүүчү суу	iʧyyʧy suu
mineral water	минерал суусу	mineral suusu

still (adj)	газсыз	gazsız
carbonated (adj)	газдалган	gazdalgan
sparkling (adj)	газы менен	gazı menen
ice	муз	muz
with ice	музу менен	muzu menen

| non-alcoholic (adj) | алкоголсуз | alkogolsuz |
| soft drink | алкоголсуз ичимдик | alkogolsuz iʧimdik |

| refreshing drink | суусундук | suusunduk |
| lemonade | лимонад | limonad |

liquors	спирт ичимдиктери	spirt itʃimdikteri
wine	шарап	ʃarap
white wine	ак шарап	ak ʃarap
red wine	кызыл шарап	kızıl ʃarap

liqueur	ликёр	likʲor
champagne	шампан	ʃampan
vermouth	вермут	vermut

whiskey	виски	viski
vodka	арак	arak
gin	джин	dʒin
cognac	коньяк	konjak
rum	ром	rom

coffee	кофе	kofe
black coffee	кара кофе	kara kofe
coffee with milk	сүттөлгөн кофе	syttølgøn kofe
cappuccino	капучино	kaputʃino
instant coffee	эрүүчү кофе	eryytʃy kofe

milk	сүт	syt
cocktail	коктейль	koktejlʲ
milkshake	сүт коктейли	syt koktejli

juice	шире	ʃire
tomato juice	томат ширеси	tomat ʃiresi
orange juice	апельсин ширеси	apelʲsin ʃiresi
freshly squeezed juice	түз сыгылып алынган шире	tyz sıgılıp alıngan ʃire

beer	сыра	sıra
light beer	ачык сыра	atʃık sıra
dark beer	коңур сыра	koŋur sıra

tea	чай	tʃaj
black tea	кара чай	kara tʃaj
green tea	жашыл чай	dʒaʃıl tʃaj

54. Vegetables

| vegetables | жашылча | dʒaʃıltʃa |
| greens | көк чөп | køk tʃøp |

tomato	помидор	pomidor
cucumber	бадыраң	badıraŋ
carrot	сабиз	sabiz

potato	картошка	kartoʃka
onion	пияз	pijaz
garlic	сарымсак	sarımsak

cabbage	капуста	kapusta
cauliflower	гүлдүү капуста	gyldyy kapusta
Brussels sprouts	брюссель капустасы	brʉsselʲ kapustası
broccoli	брокколи капустасы	brokkoli kapustası

beet	кызылча	kızıltʃa
eggplant	баклажан	bakladʒan
zucchini	кабачок	kabatʃok
pumpkin	ашкабак	aʃkabak
turnip	шалгам	ʃalgam

parsley	петрушка	petruʃka
dill	укроп	ukrop
lettuce	салат	salat
celery	сельдерей	selʲderej
asparagus	спаржа	spardʒa
spinach	шпинат	ʃpinat

pea	нокот	nokot
beans	буурчак	buurtʃak
corn (maize)	жүгөрү	dʒygøry
kidney bean	төө буурчак	tøø buurtʃak

bell pepper	таттуу перец	tattuu perets
radish	шалгам	ʃalgam
artichoke	артишок	artiʃok

55. Fruits. Nuts

fruit	мөмө	mømø
apple	алма	alma
pear	алмурут	almurut
lemon	лимон	limon
orange	апельсин	apelʲsin
strawberry (garden ~)	кулпунай	kulpunaj

mandarin	мандарин	mandarin
plum	кара өрүк	kara øryk
peach	шабдаалы	ʃabdaalı
apricot	өрүк	øryk
raspberry	дан куурай	dan kuuraj
pineapple	ананас	ananas

banana	банан	banan
watermelon	арбуз	arbuz
grape	жүзүм	dʒyzym

sour cherry	алча	altʃa
sweet cherry	гилас	gilas
melon	коон	koon

grapefruit	грейпфрут	grejpfrut
avocado	авокадо	avokado
papaya	папайя	papaja
mango	манго	mango
pomegranate	анар	anar

redcurrant	кызыл карагат	kızıl karagat
blackcurrant	кара карагат	kara karagat
gooseberry	крыжовник	krıdʒovnik
bilberry	кара моюл	kara mojʉl
blackberry	кара бүлдүркөн	kara byldyrkøn

raisin	мейиз	mejiz
fig	анжир	andʒir
date	курма	kurma

peanut	арахис	araχis
almond	бадам	badam
walnut	жаңгак	dʒaŋgak
hazelnut	токой жаңгагы	tokoj dʒaŋgagı
coconut	кокос жаңгагы	kokos dʒaŋgagı
pistachios	мисте	miste

56. Bread. Candy

bakers' confectionery (pastry)	кондитер азыктары	konditer azıktarı
bread	нан	nan
cookies	печенье	petʃenje

chocolate (n)	шоколад	ʃokolad
chocolate (as adj)	шоколаддан	ʃokoladdan
candy (wrapped)	конфета	konfeta

| cake (e.g., cupcake) | пирожное | pirodʒnoe |
| cake (e.g., birthday ~) | торт | tort |

| pie (e.g., apple ~) | пирог | pirog |
| filling (for cake, pie) | начинка | natʃinka |

| jam (whole fruit jam) | кыям | kıjam |
| marmalade | мармелад | marmelad |

wafers	вафли	vafli
ice-cream	бал муздак	bal muzdak
pudding	пудинг	puding

57. Spices

salt	туз	tuz
salty (adj)	туздуу	tuzduu
to salt (vt)	туздоо	tuzdoo

black pepper	кара мурч	kara murtʃ
red pepper (milled ~)	кызыл калемпир	kızıl kalempir
mustard	горчица	gortʃitsa
horseradish	хрен	χren

condiment	татымал	tatımal
spice	татымал	tatımal
sauce	соус	sous
vinegar	уксус	uksus

anise	анис	anis
basil	райхон	rajχon
cloves	гвоздика	gvozdika
ginger	имбирь	imbirʲ
coriander	кориандр	koriandr
cinnamon	корица	koritsa

sesame	кунжут	kundʒut
bay leaf	лавр жалбырагы	lavr dʒalbıragı
paprika	паприка	paprika
caraway	зира	zira
saffron	заапаран	zaaparan

PERSONAL INFORMATION. FAMILY

58. Personal information. Forms

name (first name)	аты	atı
surname (last name)	фамилиясы	familijası
date of birth	төрөлгөн күнү	tørølgøn kyny
place of birth	туулган жери	tuulgan dʒeri
nationality	улуту	ulutu
place of residence	жашаган жери	dʒaʃagan dʒeri
country	өлкө	ølkø
profession (occupation)	кесиби	kesibi
gender, sex	жынысы	dʒınısı
height	бою	bojʉ
weight	салмак	salmak

59. Family members. Relatives

mother	эне	ene
father	ата	ata
son	уул	uul
daughter	кыз	kız
younger daughter	кичүү кыз	kitʃyy kız
younger son	кичүү уул	kitʃyy uul
eldest daughter	улуу кыз	uluu kız
eldest son	улуу уул	uluu uul
brother	бир тууган	bir tuugan
elder brother	байке	bajke
younger brother	ини	ini
sister	бир тууган	bir tuugan
elder sister	эже	edʒe
younger sister	сиңди	siŋdi
cousin (masc.)	атасы же энеси бир тууган	atası dʒe enesi bir tuugan
cousin (fem.)	атасы же энеси бир тууган	atası dʒe enesi bir tuugan
mom, mommy	апа	apa
dad, daddy	ата	ata

parents	ата-эне	ata-ene
child	бала	bala
children	балдар	baldar
grandmother	чоң апа	ʧoŋ apa
grandfather	чоң ата	ʧoŋ ata
grandson	небере бала	nebere bala
granddaughter	небере кыз	nebere kɪz
grandchildren	неберелер	nebereler
uncle	таяке	tajake
aunt	таяже	tajadʒe
nephew	ини	ini
niece	жээн	dʒeen
mother-in-law (wife's mother)	кайын эне	kajɪn ene
father-in-law (husband's father)	кайын ата	kajɪn ata
son-in-law (daughter's husband)	күйөө бала	kyjøø bala
stepmother	өгөй эне	øgøj ene
stepfather	өгөй ата	øgøj ata
infant	эмчектеги бала	emʧektegi bala
baby (infant)	ымыркай	ɪmɪrkaj
little boy, kid	бөбөк	bøbøk
wife	аял	ajal
husband	эр	er
spouse (husband)	күйөө	kyjøø
spouse (wife)	зайып	zajɪp
married (masc.)	аялы бар	ajalɪ bar
married (fem.)	күйөөдө	kyjøødø
single (unmarried)	бойдок	bojdok
bachelor	бойдок	bojdok
divorced (masc.)	ажырашкан	adʒɪraʃkan
widow	жесир	dʒesir
widower	жесир	dʒesir
relative	тууган	tuugan
close relative	жакын тууган	dʒakɪn tuugan
distant relative	алыс тууган	alɪs tuugan
relatives	бир тууган	bir tuugan
orphan (boy or girl)	жетим	dʒetim
guardian (of a minor)	камкорчу	kamkorʧu
to adopt (a boy)	уул кылып асырап алуу	uul kɪlɪp asɪrap aluu
to adopt (a girl)	кыз кылып асырап алуу	kɪz kɪlɪp asɪrap aluu

60. Friends. Coworkers

friend (masc.)	дос	dos
friend (fem.)	курбу	kurbu
friendship	достук	dostuk
to be friends	достошуу	dostoʃuu
buddy (masc.)	шерик	ʃerik
buddy (fem.)	шерик кыз	ʃerik kız
partner	өнөктөш	ønøktøʃ
chief (boss)	башчы	baʃtʃı
superior (n)	башчы	baʃtʃı
owner, proprietor	кожоюн	kodʒodʒun
subordinate (n)	кол астындагы	kol astındagı
colleague	кесиптеш	kesipteʃ
acquaintance (person)	тааныш	taanıʃ
fellow traveler	жолдош	dʒoldoʃ
classmate	классташ	klasstaʃ
neighbor (masc.)	кошуна	koʃuna
neighbor (fem.)	кошуна	koʃuna
neighbors	кошуналар	koʃunalar

HUMAN BODY. MEDICINE

61. Head

head	баш	baʃ
face	бет	bet
nose	мурун	murun
mouth	ооз	ooz
eye	көз	køz
eyes	көздөр	køzdør
pupil	карек	karek
eyebrow	каш	kaʃ
eyelash	кирпик	kirpik
eyelid	кабак	kabak
tongue	тил	til
tooth	тиш	tiʃ
lips	эриндер	erinder
cheekbones	бет сөөгү	bet søøgy
gum	тиш эти	tiʃ eti
palate	таңдай	taŋdaj
nostrils	мурун тешиги	murun teʃigi
chin	ээк	eek
jaw	жаак	dʒaak
cheek	бет	bet
forehead	чеке	tʃeke
temple	чыкый	tʃɪkɪj
ear	кулак	kulak
back of the head	желке	dʒelke
neck	моюн	mojʉn
throat	тамак	tamak
hair	чач	tʃatʃ
hairstyle	чач жасоо	tʃatʃ dʒasoo
haircut	чач кыркуу	tʃatʃ kɪrkuu
wig	парик	parik
mustache	мурут	murut
beard	сакал	sakal
to have (a beard, etc.)	мурут коюу	murut kojʉu
braid	өрүм чач	ørym tʃatʃ
sideburns	бакенбарда	bakenbarda
red-haired (adj)	сары	sarı

gray (hair)	ак чачтуу	ak tʃatʃtuu
bald (adj)	таз	taz
bald patch	кашка	kaʃka

| ponytail | куйрук | kujruk |
| bangs | көкүл | køkyl |

62. Human body

| hand | беш манжа | beʃ mandʒa |
| arm | кол | kol |

finger	манжа	mandʒa
toe	манжа	mandʒa
thumb	бармак	barmak
little finger	чыпалак	tʃɪpalak
nail	тырмак	tırmak

fist	муштум	muʃtum
palm	алакан	alakan
wrist	билек	bilek
forearm	каруу	karuu
elbow	чыканак	tʃıkanak
shoulder	ийин	ijin

leg	бут	but
foot	таман	taman
knee	тизе	tize
calf (part of leg)	балтыр	baltır
hip	сан	san
heel	согончок	sogontʃok

body	дене	dene
stomach	курсак	kursak
chest	төш	tøʃ
breast	эмчек	emtʃek
flank	каптал	kaptal
back	арка жон	arka dʒon
lower back	бел	bel
waist	бел	bel

navel (belly button)	киндик	kindik
buttocks	жамбаш	dʒambaʃ
bottom	көчүк	køtʃyk

beauty mark	мең	meŋ
birthmark (café au lait spot)	кал	kal
tattoo	татуировка	tatuirovka
scar	тырык	tırık

63. Diseases

sickness	оору	ooru
to be sick	ооруу	ooruu
health	ден-соолук	den-sooluk
runny nose (coryza)	мурдунан суу агуу	murdunan suu aguu
tonsillitis	ангина	angina
cold (illness)	суук тийүү	suuk tijyy
to catch a cold	суук тийгизип алуу	suuk tijgizip aluu
bronchitis	бронхит	bronχit
pneumonia	кабыргадан сезгенүү	kabırgadan sezgenyy
flu, influenza	сасык тумоо	sasık tumoo
nearsighted (adj)	алыстан көрө албоо	alıstan kørø alboo
farsighted (adj)	жакындан көрө албоо	dʒakından kørø alboo
strabismus (crossed eyes)	кылый көздүүлүк	kılıj køzdyylyk
cross-eyed (adj)	кылый көздүүлүк	kılıj køzdyylyk
cataract	челкөз	tʃelkøz
glaucoma	глаукома	glaukoma
stroke	мээге кан куюлуу	meege kan kujuluu
heart attack	инфаркт	infarkt
myocardial infarction	инфаркт миокарда	infarkt miokarda
paralysis	шал	ʃal
to paralyze (vt)	шал болуу	ʃal boluu
allergy	аллергия	allergija
asthma	астма	astma
diabetes	диабет	diabet
toothache	тиш оорусу	tiʃ oorusu
caries	кариес	karies
diarrhea	ич өткү	itʃ øtky
constipation	ич катуу	itʃ katuu
stomach upset	ич бузулгандык	itʃ buzulgandık
food poisoning	ууլануу	uulanuu
to get food poisoning	ууланuu	uulanuu
arthritis	артрит	artrit
rickets	итий	itij
rheumatism	кызыл жүгүрүк	kızıl dʒygyryk
atherosclerosis	атеросклероз	ateroskleroz
gastritis	карын сезгенүүсу	karın sezgenyysu
appendicitis	аппендицит	appenditsit
cholecystitis	холецистит	χoletsistit
ulcer	жара	dʒara
measles	кызылча	kızıltʃa

rubella (German measles)	кызамык	kızamık
jaundice	сарык	sarık
hepatitis	гепатит	gepatit
schizophrenia	шизофрения	ʃizofrenija
rabies (hydrophobia)	кутурма	kuturma
neurosis	невроз	nevroz
concussion	мээнин чайкалышы	meenin tʃajkalıʃı
cancer	рак	rak
sclerosis	склероз	skleroz
multiple sclerosis	жайылган склероз	dʒajılgan skleroz
alcoholism	аракечтик	araketʃtik
alcoholic (n)	аракеч	araketʃ
syphilis	котон жара	koton dʒara
AIDS	СПИД	spid
tumor	шишик	ʃiʃik
malignant (adj)	залалдуу	zalalduu
benign (adj)	залалсыз	zalalsız
fever	безгек	bezgek
malaria	безгек	bezgek
gangrene	кабыз	kabız
seasickness	деңиз оорусу	deŋiz oorusu
epilepsy	талма	talma
epidemic	эпидемия	epidemija
typhus	келте	kelte
tuberculosis	кургак учук	kurgak utʃuk
cholera	холера	χolera
plague (bubonic ~)	кара тумоо	kara tumoo

64. Symptoms. Treatments. Part 1

symptom	белги	belgi
temperature	дене табынын көтөрүлүшү	dene tabınin køtørylyʃy
high temperature (fever)	жогорку температура	dʒogorku temperatura
pulse (heartbeat)	тамыр кагышы	tamır kagıʃı
dizziness (vertigo)	баш айлануу	baʃ ajlanuu
hot (adj)	ысык	ısık
shivering	чыйрыгуу	tʃıjrıguu
pale (e.g., ~ face)	купкуу	kupkuu
cough	жөтөл	dʒøtøl
to cough (vi)	жөтөлүү	dʒøtølyy
to sneeze (vi)	чүчкүрүү	tʃytʃkyryy

| faint | эси оо | esi oo |
| to faint (vi) | эси ооп жыгылуу | esi oop dʒɪgɪluu |

bruise (hématome)	көк-ала	køk-ala
bump (lump)	шишик	ʃiʃik
to bang (bump)	урунуп алуу	urunup aluu
contusion (bruise)	көгөртүп алуу	køgørtyp aluu
to get a bruise	көгөртүп алуу	køgørtyp aluu

to limp (vi)	аксоо	aksoo
dislocation	муундун чыгып кетүүсү	muundun tʃɪgɪp ketyysy
to dislocate (vt)	чыгарып алуу	tʃɪgarɪp aluu
fracture	сынуу	sɪnuu
to have a fracture	сындырып алуу	sɪndɪrɪp aluu

cut (e.g., paper ~)	кесилген жер	kesilgen dʒer
to cut oneself	кесип алуу	kesip aluu
bleeding	кан кетүү	kan ketyy

| burn (injury) | күйүк | kyjyk |
| to get burned | күйгүзүп алуу | kyjgyzyp aluu |

to prick (vt)	саюу	sajʉu
to prick oneself	сайып алуу	sajɪp aluu
to injure (vt)	кокустатып алуу	kokustatɪp aluu
injury	кокустатып алуу	kokustatɪp aluu
wound	жара	dʒara
trauma	жаракат	dʒarakat

to be delirious	жөлүү	dʒølyy
to stutter (vi)	кекечтенүү	keketʃtenyy
sunstroke	күн өтүү	kyn øtyy

65. Symptoms. Treatments. Part 2

| pain, ache | оору | ooru |
| splinter (in foot, etc.) | тикен | tiken |

sweat (perspiration)	тер	ter
to sweat (perspire)	тердөө	terdøø
vomiting	кусуу	kusuu
convulsions	тарамыш карышуусу	taramɪʃ karɪʃuusu

pregnant (adj)	кош бойлуу	koʃ bojluu
to be born	төрөлүү	tørølyy
delivery, labor	төрөт	tørøt
to deliver (~ a baby)	төрөө	tørøø
abortion	бойдон түшүрүү	bojdon tyʃyryy
breathing, respiration	дем алуу	dem aluu
in-breath (inhalation)	дем алуу	dem aluu

out-breath (exhalation)	дем чыгаруу	dem tʃıgaruu
to exhale (breathe out)	дем чыгаруу	dem tʃıgaruu
to inhale (vi)	дем алуу	dem aluu
disabled person	майып	majıp
cripple	мунжу	mundʒu
drug addict	баңги	baŋgi
deaf (adj)	дүлөй	dyløj
mute (adj)	дудук	duduk
deaf mute (adj)	дудук	duduk
mad, insane (adj)	жин тийген	dʒin tijgen
madman (demented person)	жинди чалыш	dʒindi tʃalıʃ
madwoman	жинди чалыш	dʒindi tʃalıʃ
to go insane	мээси айныган	meesi ajnıgan
gene	ген	gen
immunity	иммунитет	immunitet
hereditary (adj)	тукум куучулук	tukum kuutʃuluk
congenital (adj)	тубаса	tubasa
virus	вирус	virus
microbe	микроб	mikrob
bacterium	бактерия	bakterija
infection	жугуштуу илдет	dʒuguʃtuu ildet

66. Symptoms. Treatments. Part 3

hospital	оорукана	oorukana
patient	бейтап	bejtap
diagnosis	дарт аныктоо	dart anıktoo
cure	дарылоо	dariloo
medical treatment	дарылоо	dariloo
to get treatment	дарылануу	darilanuu
to treat (~ a patient)	дарылоо	dariloo
to nurse (look after)	кароо	karoo
care (nursing ~)	кароо	karoo
operation, surgery	операция	operatsija
to bandage (head, limb)	жараны таңуу	dʒaranı taŋuu
bandaging	таңуу	taŋuu
vaccination	эмдөө	emdøø
to vaccinate (vt)	эмдөө	emdøø
injection, shot	ийне салуу	ijne saluu
to give an injection	ийне сайдыруу	ijne sajdıruu
attack	оору кармап калуу	ooru karmap kaluu

amputation	кесүү	kesyy
to amputate (vt)	кесип таштоо	kesip taʃtoo
coma	кома	koma
to be in a coma	комада болуу	komada boluu
intensive care	реанимация	reanimatsija

to recover (~ from flu)	сакаюу	sakajuu
condition (patient's ~)	абал	abal
consciousness	эсинде	esinde
memory (faculty)	эс тутум	es tutum

to pull out (tooth)	тишти жулуу	tiʃti dʒuluu
filling	пломба	plomba
to fill (a tooth)	пломба салуу	plomba saluu

| hypnosis | гипноз | gipnoz |
| to hypnotize (vt) | гипноз кылуу | gipnoz kıluu |

67. Medicine. Drugs. Accessories

medicine, drug	дары-дармек	darı-darmek
remedy	дары	darı
to prescribe (vt)	жазып берүү	dʒazıp beryy
prescription	рецепт	retsept

tablet, pill	таблетка	tabletka
ointment	май	maj
ampule	ампула	ampula
mixture, solution	аралашма	aralaʃma
syrup	сироп	sirop
capsule	пилюля	pilulʲa
powder	күкүм	kykym

gauze bandage	бинт	bint
cotton wool	пахта	paχta
iodine	йод	jod
Band-Aid	лейкопластырь	lejkoplastırʲ
eyedropper	дары тамызгыч	darı tamızgıtʃ
thermometer	градусник	gradusnik
syringe	шприц	ʃprits

| wheelchair | майып арабасы | majıp arabası |
| crutches | колтук таяк | koltuk tajak |

painkiller	оору сездирбөөчү дары	ooru sezdirbøøtʃy darı
laxative	ич алдыруучу дары	itʃ aldıruutʃu darı
spirits (ethanol)	спирт	spirt
medicinal herbs	дары чөптөр	darı tʃøptør
herbal (~ tea)	чөп чайы	tʃøp tʃajı

APARTMENT

68. Apartment

apartment	батир	batir
room	бөлмө	bølmø
bedroom	уктоочу бөлмө	uktootʃu bølmø
dining room	ашкана	aʃkana
living room	конок үйү	konok yjy
study (home office)	иш бөлмөсү	iʃ bølmøsy
entry room	кире бериш	kire beriʃ
bathroom (room with a bath or shower)	ванная	vannaja
half bath	даараткана	daaratkana
ceiling	шып	ʃɪp
floor	пол	pol
corner	бурч	burtʃ

69. Furniture. Interior

furniture	эмерек	emerek
table	стол	stol
chair	стул	stul
bed	керебет	kerebet
couch, sofa	диван	divan
armchair	олпок отургуч	olpok oturgutʃ
bookcase	китеп шкафы	kitep ʃkafɪ
shelf	текче	tektʃe
wardrobe	шкаф	ʃkaf
coat rack (wall-mounted ~)	кийим илгич	kijim ilgitʃ
coat stand	кийим илгич	kijim ilgitʃ
bureau, dresser	комод	komod
coffee table	журнал столу	dʒurnal stolu
mirror	күзгү	kyzgy
carpet	килем	kilem
rug, small carpet	килемче	kilemtʃe
fireplace	очок	otʃok
candle	шам	ʃam

candlestick	шамдал	ʃamdal
drapes	парда	parda
wallpaper	туш кагаз	tuʃ kagaz
blinds (jalousie)	жалюзи	dʒaldʒʉzi

table lamp	стол чырагы	stol tʃɪragɪ
wall lamp (sconce)	чырак	tʃɪrak
floor lamp	торшер	torʃer
chandelier	асма шам	asma ʃam

leg (of chair, table)	бут	but
armrest	чыканак такооч	tʃɪkanak takootʃ
back (backrest)	желенгуч	dʒøløŋgytʃ
drawer	суурма	suurma

70. Bedding

bedclothes	шейшеп	ʃejʃep
pillow	жаздык	dʒazdɪk
pillowcase	жаздык кап	dʒazdɪk kap
duvet, comforter	жууркан	dʒuurkan
sheet	шейшеп	ʃejʃep
bedspread	жапкыч	dʒapkɪtʃ

71. Kitchen

kitchen	ашкана	aʃkana
gas	газ	gaz
gas stove (range)	газ плитасы	gaz plitasɪ
electric stove	электр плитасы	elektr plitasɪ
oven	духовка	duxovka
microwave oven	микротолкун меши	mikrotolkun meʃi

refrigerator	муздаткыч	muzdatkɪtʃ
freezer	тоңдургуч	toŋdurgutʃ
dishwasher	идиш жуучу машина	idiʃ dʒuutʃu maʃina

meat grinder	эт туурагыч	et tuuragɪtʃ
juicer	шире сыккыч	ʃire sɪkkɪtʃ
toaster	тостер	toster
mixer	миксер	mikser

coffee machine	кофе кайнаткыч	kofe kajnatkɪtʃ
coffee pot	кофе кайнатуучу идиш	kofe kajnatuutʃu idiʃ
coffee grinder	кофе майдалагыч	kofe majdalagɪtʃ

| kettle | чайнек | tʃajnek |
| teapot | чайнек | tʃajnek |

| lid | капкак | kapkak |
| tea strainer | чыпка | tʃɪpka |

spoon	кашык	kaʃɪk
teaspoon	чай кашык	tʃaj kaʃɪk
soup spoon	аш кашык	aʃ kaʃɪk
fork	вилка	vilka
knife	бычак	bɪtʃak

tableware (dishes)	идиш-аяк	idiʃ-ajak
plate (dinner ~)	табак	tabak
saucer	табак	tabak

shot glass	рюмка	rʉmka
glass (tumbler)	ыстакан	ɪstakan
cup	чөйчөк	tʃøjtʃøk

sugar bowl	кум шекер салгыч	kum ʃeker salgɪtʃ
salt shaker	туз салгыч	tuz salgɪtʃ
pepper shaker	мурч салгыч	murtʃ salgɪtʃ
butter dish	май салгыч	maj salgɪtʃ

stock pot (soup pot)	мискей	miskej
frying pan (skillet)	табак	tabak
ladle	чөмүч	tʃømytʃ
colander	депкир	depkir
tray (serving ~)	батыныс	batɪnɪs

bottle	бөтөлкө	bøtølkø
jar (glass)	банка	banka
can	банка	banka

bottle opener	ачкыч	atʃkɪtʃ
can opener	ачкыч	atʃkɪtʃ
corkscrew	штопор	ʃtopor
filter	чыпка	tʃɪpka
to filter (vt)	чыпкалоо	tʃɪpkaloo

| trash, garbage (food waste, etc.) | таштанды | taʃtandɪ |
| trash can (kitchen ~) | таштанды чака | taʃtandɪ tʃaka |

72. Bathroom

bathroom	ванная	vannaja
water	суу	suu
faucet	чорго	tʃorgo
hot water	ысык суу	ɪsɪk suu
cold water	муздак суу	muzdak suu
toothpaste	тиш пастасы	tiʃ pastasɪ

| to brush one's teeth | тиш жуу | tiʃ dʒuu |
| toothbrush | тиш щёткасы | tiʃ ʃtʃotkası |

to shave (vi)	кырынуу	kırınuu
shaving foam	кырынуу үчүн көбүк	kırınuu ytʃyn købyk
razor	устара	ustara

to wash (one's hands, etc.)	жуу	dʒuu
to take a bath	жуунуу	dʒuunuu
shower	душ	duʃ
to take a shower	душка түшүү	duʃka tyʃyy

bathtub	ванна	vanna
toilet (toilet bowl)	унитаз	unitaz
sink (washbasin)	раковина	rakovina

| soap | самын | samın |
| soap dish | самын салгыч | samın salgıtʃ |

sponge	губка	gubka
shampoo	шампунь	ʃampunʲ
towel	сүлгү	sylgy
bathrobe	халат	χalat

laundry (laundering)	кир жуу	kir dʒuu
washing machine	кир жуучу машина	kir dʒuutʃu maʃina
to do the laundry	кир жуу	kir dʒuu
laundry detergent	кир жуучу порошок	kir dʒuutʃu poroʃok

73. Household appliances

TV set	сыналгы	sınalgı
tape recorder	магнитофон	magnitofon
VCR (video recorder)	видеомагнитофон	videomagnitofon
radio	үналгы	ynalgı
player (CD, MP3, etc.)	плеер	pleer

video projector	видеопроектор	videoproektor
home movie theater	үй кинотеатры	yj kinoteatrı
DVD player	DVD ойноткуч	dividi ojnotkutʃ
amplifier	күчөткүч	kytʃøtkytʃ
video game console	оюн приставкасы	ojʉn pristavkası

video camera	видеокамера	videokamera
camera (photo)	фотоаппарат	fotoapparat
digital camera	санарип камерасы	sanarip kamerası

vacuum cleaner	чаң соргуч	tʃaŋ sorgutʃ
iron (e.g., steam ~)	үтүк	ytyk
ironing board	үтүктөөчү тактай	ytyktøøtʃy taktaj

telephone	**телефон**	telefon
cell phone	**мобилдик**	mobildik
typewriter	**машинка**	maʃinka
sewing machine	**кийим тигүүчү машинка**	kijim tigyytʃy maʃinka
microphone	**микрофон**	mikrofon
headphones	**кулакчын**	kulaktʃin
remote control (TV)	**пульт**	pulʹt
CD, compact disc	**CD, компакт-диск**	sidi, kompakt-disk
cassette, tape	**кассета**	kasseta
vinyl record	**пластинка**	plastinka

THE EARTH. WEATHER

74. Outer space

space	космос	kosmos
space (as adj)	космос	kosmos
outer space	космос мейкиндиги	kosmos mejkindigi
world	дүйнө	dyjnø
universe	аалам	aalam
galaxy	галактика	galaktika
star	жылдыз	dʒıldız
constellation	жылдыздар	dʒıldızdar
planet	планета	planeta
satellite	жолдош	dʒoldoʃ
meteorite	метеорит	meteorit
comet	комета	kometa
asteroid	астероид	asteroid
orbit	орбита	orbita
to revolve (~ around the Earth)	айлануу	ajlanuu
atmosphere	атмосфера	atmosfera
the Sun	күн	kyn
solar system	күн системасы	kyn sisteması
solar eclipse	күндүн тутулушу	kyndyn tutuluʃu
the Earth	Жер	dʒer
the Moon	Ай	aj
Mars	Марс	mars
Venus	Венера	venera
Jupiter	Юпитер	jʉpiter
Saturn	Сатурн	saturn
Mercury	Меркурий	merkurij
Uranus	Уран	uran
Neptune	Нептун	neptun
Pluto	Плутон	pluton
Milky Way	Саманчынын жолу	samantʃının dʒolu
Great Bear (Ursa Major)	Чоң Жетиген	tʃoŋ dʒetigen
North Star	Полярдык Жылдыз	polʲardık dʒıldız

Martian	марсианин	marsianin
extraterrestrial (n)	инопланетянин	inoplanet'anin
alien	келгин	kelgin
flying saucer	учуучу табак	utʃuutʃu tabak

spaceship	космос кемеси	kosmos kemesi
space station	орбитадагы станция	orbitadagı stantsija
blast-off	старт	start

engine	кыймылдаткыч	kıjmıldatkıtʃ
nozzle	сопло	soplo
fuel	күйүүчү май	kyjyytʃy may

cockpit, flight deck	кабина	kabina
antenna	антенна	antenna
porthole	иллюминатор	illuminator
solar panel	күн батареясы	kyn batarejası
spacesuit	скафандр	skafandr

weightlessness	салмаксыздык	salmaksızdık
oxygen	кислород	kislorod

docking (in space)	жалгаштыруу	dʒalgaʃtıruu
to dock (vi, vt)	жалгаштыруу	dʒalgaʃtıruu

observatory	обсерватория	observatorija
telescope	телескоп	teleskop
to observe (vt)	байкоо	bajkoo
to explore (vt)	изилдөө	izildøø

75. The Earth

the Earth	Жер	dʒer
the globe (the Earth)	жер шары	dʒer ʃarı
planet	планета	planeta

atmosphere	атмосфера	atmosfera
geography	география	geografija
nature	табийгат	tabijgat

globe (table ~)	глобус	globus
map	карта	karta
atlas	атлас	atlas

Europe	Европа	evropa
Asia	Азия	azija
Africa	Африка	afrika
Australia	Австралия	avstralija
America	Америка	amerika
North America	Северная Америка	severnaja amerika

South America	Южная Америка	jʊdʒnaja amerika
Antarctica	Антарктида	antarktida
the Arctic	Арктика	arktika

76. Cardinal directions

north	түндүк	tyndyk
to the north	түндүккө	tyndykkø
in the north	түндүктө	tyndyktø
northern (adj)	түндүк	tyndyk

south	түштүк	tyʃtyk
to the south	түштүккө	tyʃtykkø
in the south	түштүктө	tyʃtyktø
southern (adj)	түштүк	tyʃtyk

west	батыш	batıʃ
to the west	батышка	batıʃka
in the west	батышта	batıʃta
western (adj)	батыш	batıʃ

east	чыгыш	ʧıgıʃ
to the east	чыгышка	ʧıgıʃka
in the east	чыгышта	ʧıgıʃta
eastern (adj)	чыгыш	ʧıgıʃ

77. Sea. Ocean

sea	деңиз	deŋiz
ocean	мухит	muχit
gulf (bay)	булуң	buluŋ
straits	кысык	kısık

| land (solid ground) | жер | dʒer |
| continent (mainland) | материк | materik |

island	арал	aral
peninsula	жарым арал	dʒarım aral
archipelago	архипелаг	arχipelag

bay, cove	булуң	buluŋ
harbor	гавань	gavanʲ
lagoon	лагуна	laguna
cape	тумшук	tumʃuk

atoll	атолл	atoll
reef	риф	rif
coral	маржан	mardʒan

coral reef	маржан рифи	mardʒan rifi
deep (adj)	терең	tereŋ
depth (deep water)	терендик	tereŋdik
abyss	түбү жок	tyby dʒok
trench (e.g., Mariana ~)	ойдуң	ojduŋ
current (Ocean ~)	агым	agım
to surround (bathe)	курчап туруу	kurtʃap turuu
shore	жээк	dʒeek
coast	жээк	dʒeek
flow (flood tide)	суунун көтөрүлүшү	suunun køtørylyʃy
ebb (ebb tide)	суунун тартылуусу	suunun tartıluusu
shoal	тайыздык	tajızdık
bottom (~ of the sea)	суунун түбү	suunun tyby
wave	толкун	tolkun
crest (~ of a wave)	толкундун кыры	tolkundun kırı
spume (sea foam)	көбүк	købyk
storm (sea storm)	бороон чапкын	boroon tʃapkın
hurricane	бороон	boroon
tsunami	цунами	tsunami
calm (dead ~)	штиль	ʃtilʲ
quiet, calm (adj)	тынч	tıntʃ
pole	уюл	ujʉl
polar (adj)	полярдык	polʲardık
latitude	кеңдик	keŋdik
longitude	узундук	uzunduk
parallel	параллель	parallelʲ
equator	экватор	ekvator
sky	асман	asman
horizon	горизонт	gorizont
air	аба	aba
lighthouse	маяк	majak
to dive (vi)	сүңгүү	syŋgyy
to sink (ab. boat)	чөгүп кетүү	tʃøgyp ketyy
treasures	казына	kazına

78. Seas' and Oceans' names

Atlantic Ocean	Атлантика мухити	atlantika muχiti
Indian Ocean	Индия мухити	indija muχiti
Pacific Ocean	Тынч мухити	tıntʃ muχiti
Arctic Ocean	Түндүк Муз мухити	tyndyk muz muχiti

Black Sea	Кара деңиз	kara deŋiz
Red Sea	Кызыл деңиз	kızıl deŋiz
Yellow Sea	Сары деңиз	sarı deŋiz
White Sea	Ак деңиз	ak deŋiz

Caspian Sea	Каспий деңизи	kaspij deŋizi
Dead Sea	Өлүк деңиз	ølyk deŋiz
Mediterranean Sea	Жер Ортолук деңиз	dʒer ortoluk deŋiz

| Aegean Sea | Эгей деңизи | egej deŋizi |
| Adriatic Sea | Адриатика деңизи | adriatika deŋizi |

Arabian Sea	Аравия деңизи	aravija deŋizi
Sea of Japan	Япон деңизи	japon deŋizi
Bering Sea	Беринг деңизи	bering deŋizi
South China Sea	Түштүк-Кытай деңизи	tyʃtyk-kıtaj deŋizi

Coral Sea	Маржан деңизи	mardʒan deŋizi
Tasman Sea	Тасман деңизи	tasman deŋizi
Caribbean Sea	Кариб деңизи	karib deŋizi

| Barents Sea | Баренц деңизи | barents deŋizi |
| Kara Sea | Карск деңизи | karsk deŋizi |

North Sea	Түндүк деңиз	tyndyk deŋiz
Baltic Sea	Балтика деңизи	baltika deŋizi
Norwegian Sea	Норвегиялык деңизи	norvegijalık deŋizi

79. Mountains

mountain	тоо	too
mountain range	тоо тизмеги	too tizmegi
mountain ridge	тоо кыркалары	too kırkaları

summit, top	чоку	tʃoku
peak	чоку	tʃoku
foot (~ of the mountain)	тоо этеги	too etegi
slope (mountainside)	эңкейиш	eŋkejiʃ

volcano	вулкан	vulkan
active volcano	күйүп жаткан	kyjyp dʒatkan
dormant volcano	өчүп калган вулкан	øtʃyp kalgan vulkan

eruption	атырылып чыгуу	atırılıp tʃıguu
crater	кратер	krater
magma	магма	magma
lava	лава	lava
molten (~ lava)	кызыган	kızıgan
canyon	каньон	kanʲon
gorge	капчыгай	kaptʃıgaj

| crevice | жарака | dʒaraka |
| abyss (chasm) | жар | dʒar |

pass, col	ашуу	aʃuu
plateau	дөңсөө	døŋsøø
cliff	зоока	zooka
hill	дөбө	døbø

glacier	муз	muz
waterfall	шаркыратма	ʃarkıratma
geyser	гейзер	gejzer
lake	көл	køl

plain	түздүк	tyzdyk
landscape	теребел	terebel
echo	жаңырык	dʒaŋırık

alpinist	альпинист	alʲpinist
rock climber	скалолаз	skalolaz
to conquer (in climbing)	багындыруу	bagındıruu
climb (an easy ~)	тоонун чокусуна чыгуу	toonun tʃokusuna tʃıguu

80. Mountains names

The Alps	Альп тоолору	alʲp tooloru
Mont Blanc	Монблан	monblan
The Pyrenees	Пиреней тоолору	pirenej tooloru

The Carpathians	Карпат тоолору	karpat tooloru
The Ural Mountains	Урал тоолору	ural tooloru
The Caucasus Mountains	Кавказ тоолору	kavkaz tooloru
Mount Elbrus	Эльбрус	elʲbrus

The Altai Mountains	Алтай тоолору	altaj tooloru
The Tian Shan	Тянь-Шань	tjanʲ-ʃanʲ
The Pamir Mountains	Памир тоолору	pamir tooloru
The Himalayas	Гималай тоолору	gimalaj tooloru
Mount Everest	Эверест	everest

| The Andes | Анд тоолору | and tooloru |
| Mount Kilimanjaro | Килиманджаро | kilimandʒaro |

81. Rivers

river	дарыя	darıja
spring (natural source)	булак	bulak
riverbed (river channel)	сай	saj
basin (river valley)	бассейн	bassejn

to flow into …	… куюу	… kujʉu
tributary	куйма	kujma
bank (of river)	жээк	dʒeek

current (stream)	агым	agım
downstream (adv)	агым боюнча	agım bojʉntʃa
upstream (adv)	агымга каршы	agımga karʃı

inundation	ташкын	taʃkın
flooding	суу ташкыны	suu taʃkını
to overflow (vi)	дайранын ташышы	dajranın taʃıʃı
to flood (vt)	суу каптоо	suu kaptoo

| shallow (shoal) | тайыздык | tajızdık |
| rapids | босого | bosogo |

dam	тогоон	togoon
canal	канал	kanal
reservoir (artificial lake)	суу сактагыч	suu saktagıtʃ
sluice, lock	шлюз	ʃlʉz

water body (pond, etc.)	көлмө	kølmø
swamp (marshland)	саз	saz
bog, marsh	баткак	batkak
whirlpool	айлампа	ajlampa

stream (brook)	суу	suu
drinking (ab. water)	ичилчү суу	itʃiltʃy suu
fresh (~ water)	тузсуз	tuzsuz

| ice | муз | muz |
| to freeze over (ab. river, etc.) | тоңуп калуу | toŋup kaluu |

82. Rivers' names

| Seine | Сена | sena |
| Loire | Луара | luara |

Thames	Темза	temza
Rhine	Рейн	rejn
Danube	Дунай	dunaj

Volga	Волга	volga
Don	Дон	don
Lena	Лена	lena

Yellow River	Хуанхэ	χuanχe
Yangtze	Янцзы	jantszı
Mekong	Меконг	mekong

Ganges	Ганг	gang
Nile River	Нил	nil
Congo River	Конго	kongo
Okavango River	Окаванго	okavango
Zambezi River	Замбези	zambezi
Limpopo River	Лимпопо	limpopo
Mississippi River	Миссисипи	missisipi

83. Forest

forest, wood	токой	tokoj
forest (as adj)	токойлуу	tokojluu
thick forest	чытырман токой	tʃɪtɪrman tokoj
grove	токойчо	tokojtʃo
forest clearing	аянт	ajant
thicket	бадал	badal
scrubland	бадал	badal
footpath (troddenpath)	чыйыр жол	tʃɪjɪr dʒol
gully	жар	dʒar
tree	дарак	darak
leaf	жалбырак	dʒalbɪrak
leaves (foliage)	жалбырак	dʒalbɪrak
fall of leaves	жалбырак түшүү мезгили	dʒalbɪrak tyʃyy mezgili
to fall (ab. leaves)	түшүү	tyʃyy
top (of the tree)	чоку	tʃoku
branch	бутак	butak
bough	бутак	butak
bud (on shrub, tree)	бүчүр	bytʃyr
needle (of pine tree)	ийне	ijne
pine cone	тобурчак	toburtʃak
tree hollow	көндөй	køŋdøj
nest	уя	uja
burrow (animal hole)	ийин	ijin
trunk	сөңгөк	søŋgøk
root	тамыр	tamɪr
bark	кыртыш	kɪrtɪʃ
moss	мох	moχ
to uproot (remove trees or tree stumps)	дүмүрүн казуу	dymyryn kazuu
to chop down	кыюу	kɪjʉu

| to deforest (vt) | токойду кыюу | tokojdu kıjuu |
| tree stump | дүмүр | dymyr |

campfire	от	ot
forest fire	өрт	ørt
to extinguish (vt)	өчүрүү	øʧyryy

forest ranger	токойчу	tokojʧu
protection	өсүмдүктөрдү коргоо	øsymdyktørdy korgoo
to protect (~ nature)	сактоо	saktoo
poacher	браконьер	brakonjer
steel trap	капкан	kapkan

to pick (mushrooms)	терүү	teryy
to pick (berries)	терүү	teryy
to lose one's way	адашып кетүү	adaʃıp ketyy

84. Natural resources

natural resources	жаратылыш байлыктары	ʤaratılıʃ bajlıktarı
minerals	пайдалуу кендер	pajdaluu kender
deposits	кен	ken
field (e.g., oilfield)	кендүү жер	kendyy ʤer

to mine (extract)	казуу	kazuu
mining (extraction)	казуу	kazuu
ore	кен	ken
mine (e.g., for coal)	шахта	ʃaxta
shaft (mine ~)	шахта	ʃaxta
miner	кенчи	kenʧi

| gas (natural ~) | газ | gaz |
| gas pipeline | газопровод | gazoprovod |

oil (petroleum)	мунайзат	munajzat
oil pipeline	мунайзар түтүгү	munajzar tytygy
oil well	мунайзат скважинасы	munajzat skvadʒinası
derrick (tower)	мунайзат мунарасы	munajzat munarası
tanker	танкер	tanker

sand	кум	kum
limestone	акиташ	akitaʃ
gravel	шагыл	ʃagıl
peat	торф	torf
clay	ылай	ılaj
coal	көмүр	kømyr

| iron (ore) | темир | temir |
| gold | алтын | altın |

silver	күмүш	kymyʃ
nickel	никель	nikelʲ
copper	жез	dʒez

zinc	цинк	tsınk
manganese	марганец	marganets
mercury	сымап	sımap
lead	коргошун	korgoʃun

mineral	минерал	mineral
crystal	кристалл	kristall
marble	мрамор	mramor
uranium	уран	uran

85. Weather

weather	аба-ырайы	aba-ırajı
weather forecast	аба-ырайы боюнча маалымат	aba-ırajı bojuntʃa maalımat
temperature	температура	temperatura
thermometer	термометр	termometr
barometer	барометр	barometr

| humid (adj) | нымдуу | nımduu |
| humidity | ным | nım |

heat (extreme ~)	ысык	ısık
hot (torrid)	кыйын ысык	kıjın ısık
it's hot	ысык	ısık

| it's warm | жылуу | dʒıluu |
| warm (moderately hot) | жылуу | dʒıluu |

| it's cold | суук | suuk |
| cold (adj) | суук | suuk |

sun	күн	kyn
to shine (vi)	күн тийүү	kyn tijyy
sunny (day)	күн ачык	kyn atʃık
to come up (vi)	чыгуу	tʃıguu
to set (vi)	батуу	batuu

cloud	булут	bulut
cloudy (adj)	булуттуу	buluttuu
rain cloud	булут	bulut
somber (gloomy)	күн бүркөк	kyn byrkøk

rain	жамгыр	dʒamgır
it's raining	жамгыр жаап жатат	dʒamgır dʒaap dʒatat
rainy (~ day, weather)	жаандуу	dʒaanduu

to drizzle (vi)	дыбыратуу	dıbıratuu
pouring rain	нөшөрлөгөн жаан	nøʃørløgøn dʒaan
downpour	нөшөр	nøʃør
heavy (e.g., ~ rain)	катуу	katuu
puddle	көлчүк	køltʃyk
to get wet (in rain)	суу болуу	suu boluu

fog (mist)	туман	tuman
foggy	тумандуу	tumanduu
snow	кар	kar
it's snowing	кар жаап жатат	kar dʒaap dʒatat

86. Severe weather. Natural disasters

thunderstorm	чагылгандуу жаан	tʃagılganduu dʒaan
lightning (~ strike)	чагылган	tʃagılgan
to flash (vi)	жарк этүү	dʒark etyy

thunder	күн күркүрөө	kyn kyrkyrøø
to thunder (vi)	күн күркүрөө	kyn kyrkyrøø
it's thundering	күн күркүрөп жатат	kyn kyrkyrøp dʒatat

| hail | мөндүр | møndyr |
| it's hailing | мөндүр түшүп жатат | møndyr tyʃyp dʒatat |

| to flood (vt) | суу каптоо | suu kaptoo |
| flood, inundation | ташкын | taʃkın |

earthquake	жер титирөө	dʒer titirøø
tremor, shoke	жердин силкиниши	dʒerdin silkiniʃi
epicenter	эпицентр	epitsentr

| eruption | атырылып чыгуу | atırılıp tʃıguu |
| lava | лава | lava |

twister	куюн	kujɵn
tornado	торнадо	tornado
typhoon	тайфун	tajfun

hurricane	бороон	boroon
storm	бороон чапкын	boroon tʃapkın
tsunami	цунами	tsunami

cyclone	циклон	tsıklon
bad weather	жаан-чачындуу күн	dʒaan-tʃatʃınduu kyn
fire (accident)	өрт	ørt
disaster	кыйроо	kıjroo
meteorite	метеорит	meteorit
avalanche	көчкү	køtʃky
snowslide	кар көчкүсү	kar køtʃkysy

blizzard	**кар бороону**	kar boroonu
snowstorm	**бурганак**	burganak

FAUNA

87. Mammals. Predators

predator	жырткыч	dʒɯrtkɯtʃ
tiger	жолборс	dʒolbors
lion	арстан	arstan
wolf	карышкыр	karɯʃkɯr
fox	түлкү	tylky
jaguar	ягуар	jaguar
leopard	леопард	leopard
cheetah	гепард	gepard
black panther	пантера	pantera
puma	пума	puma
snow leopard	илбирс	ilbirs
lynx	сүлөөсүн	syløøsyn
coyote	койот	kojot
jackal	чөө	tʃøø
hyena	гиена	giena

88. Wild animals

animal	жаныбар	dʒanɯbar
beast (animal)	жапайы жаныбар	dʒapajɯ dʒanɯbar
squirrel	тыйын чычкан	tɯjɯn tʃɯtʃkan
hedgehog	кирпичечен	kirpitʃetʃen
hare	коен	koen
rabbit	коен	koen
badger	кашкулак	kaʃkulak
raccoon	енот	enot
hamster	хомяк	χomʲak
marmot	суур	suur
mole	момолой	momoloj
mouse	чычкан	tʃɯtʃkan
rat	келемиш	kelemiʃ
bat	жарганат	dʒarganat
ermine	арс чычкан	ars tʃɯtʃkan
sable	киш	kiʃ

marten	суусар	suusar
weasel	ласка	laska
mink	норка	norka

| beaver | кемчет | kemtʃet |
| otter | кундуз | kunduz |

horse	жылкы	dʒɪlkɪ
moose	багыш	bagɪʃ
deer	бугу	bugu
camel	төө	tøø

bison	бизон	bizon
wisent	зубр	zubr
buffalo	буйвол	bujvol

zebra	зебра	zebra
antelope	антилопа	antilopa
roe deer	элик	elik
fallow deer	лань	lanʲ
chamois	жейрен	dʒejren
wild boar	каман	kaman

whale	кит	kit
seal	тюлень	tʉlenʲ
walrus	морж	mordʒ
fur seal	деңиз мышыгы	deŋiz mɪʃɪgɪ
dolphin	дельфин	delʲfin

bear	аюу	ajʉu
polar bear	ак аюу	ak ajʉu
panda	панда	panda

monkey	маймыл	majmɪl
chimpanzee	шимпанзе	ʃimpanze
orangutan	орангутанг	orangutang
gorilla	горилла	gorilla
macaque	макака	makaka
gibbon	гиббон	gibbon

elephant	пил	pil
rhinoceros	керик	kerik
giraffe	жираф	dʒiraf
hippopotamus	бегемот	begemot

| kangaroo | кенгуру | kenguru |
| koala (bear) | коала | koala |

mongoose	мангуст	mangust
chinchilla	шиншилла	ʃinʃilla
skunk	скунс	skuns
porcupine	чүткөр	tʃʏtkør

89. Domestic animals

cat	ургаачы мышык	urgaatʃı mıʃık
tomcat	эркек мышык	erkek mıʃık
dog	ит	it
horse	жылкы	dʒılkı
stallion (male horse)	айгыр	ajgır
mare	бээ	bee
cow	уй	uj
bull	бука	buka
ox	өгүз	øgyz
sheep (ewe)	кой	koj
ram	кочкор	kotʃkor
goat	эчки	etʃki
billy goat, he-goat	теке	teke
donkey	эшек	eʃek
mule	качыр	katʃır
pig, hog	чочко	tʃotʃko
piglet	торопой	toropoj
rabbit	коен	koen
hen (chicken)	тоок	took
rooster	короз	koroz
duck	өрдөк	ørdøk
drake	эркек өрдөк	erkek ørdøk
goose	каз	kaz
tom turkey, gobbler	күрп	kyrp
turkey (hen)	ургаачы күрп	urgaatʃı kyrp
domestic animals	үй жаныбарлары	yj dʒanıbarları
tame (e.g., ~ hamster)	колго үйрөтүлгөн	kolgo yjrøtylgøn
to tame (vt)	колго үйрөтүү	kolgo yjrøtyy
to breed (vt)	өстүрүү	østyryy
farm	ферма	ferma
poultry	үй канаттулары	yj kanattuları
cattle	мал	mal
herd (cattle)	бада	bada
stable	аткана	atkana
pigpen	чочкокана	tʃotʃkokana
cowshed	уйкана	ujkana
rabbit hutch	коенкана	koenkana
hen house	тоокана	tookana

90. Birds

bird	куш	kuʃ
pigeon	көгүчкөн	køgytʃkøn
sparrow	таранчы	tarantʃı
tit (great tit)	синица	sinitsa
magpie	сагызган	sagızgan
raven	кузгун	kuzgun
crow	карга	karga
jackdaw	таан	taan
rook	чаркарга	tʃarkarga
duck	өрдөк	ørdøk
goose	каз	kaz
pheasant	кыргоол	kırgool
eagle	бүркүт	byrkyt
hawk	ителги	itelgi
falcon	шумкар	ʃumkar
vulture	жору	dʒoru
condor (Andean ~)	кондор	kondor
swan	аккуу	akkuu
crane	турна	turna
stork	илегилек	ilegilek
parrot	тотукуш	totukuʃ
hummingbird	колибри	kolibri
peacock	тоос	toos
ostrich	төө куш	tøø kuʃ
heron	көк кытан	køk kıtan
flamingo	фламинго	flamingo
pelican	биргазан	birgazan
nightingale	булбул	bulbul
swallow	чабалекей	tʃabalekej
thrush	таркылдак	tarkıldak
song thrush	сайрагыч таркылдак	sajragıtʃ tarkıldak
blackbird	кара таңдай таркылдак	kara taŋdaj tarkıldak
swift	кардыгач	kardıgatʃ
lark	торгой	torgoj
quail	бөдөнө	bødønø
woodpecker	тоңкулдак	toŋkuldak
cuckoo	күкүк	kykyk
owl	мыкый үкү	mıkıj yky
eagle owl	үкү	yky

wood grouse	керең кур	kereŋ kur
black grouse	кара кур	kara kur
partridge	кекилик	kekilik

starling	чыйырчык	ʧɯjɯrʧɯk
canary	канарейка	kanarejka
hazel grouse	токой чили	tokoj ʧili
chaffinch	зяблик	zʲablik
bullfinch	снегирь	snegirʲ

seagull	ак чардак	ak ʧardak
albatross	альбатрос	alʲbatros
penguin	пингвин	pingvin

91. Fish. Marine animals

bream	лещ	leʃʧ
carp	карп	karp
perch	окунь	okunʲ
catfish	жаян	ʤajan
pike	чортон	ʧorton

| salmon | лосось | lososʲ |
| sturgeon | осётр | osʲotr |

herring	сельдь	selʲdʲ
Atlantic salmon	сёмга	sʲomga
mackerel	скумбрия	skumbrija
flatfish	камбала	kambala

zander, pike perch	судак	sudak
cod	треска	treska
tuna	тунец	tunets
trout	форель	forelʲ

eel	угорь	ugorʲ
electric ray	скат	skat
moray eel	мурена	murena
piranha	пиранья	piranja

shark	акула	akula
dolphin	дельфин	delʲfin
whale	кит	kit

crab	краб	krab
jellyfish	медуза	meduza
octopus	сегиз бут	segiz but

| starfish | деңиз жылдызы | deŋiz ʤɯldɯzɯ |
| sea urchin | деңиз кирписи | deŋiz kirpisi |

seahorse	деңиз тайы	deŋiz tajı
oyster	устрица	ustritsa
shrimp	креветка	krevetka
lobster	омар	omar
spiny lobster	лангуст	langust

92. Amphibians. Reptiles

snake	жылан	dʒılan
venomous (snake)	уулуу	uuluu

viper	кара чаар жылан	kara tʃaar dʒılan
cobra	кобра	kobra
python	питон	piton
boa	удав	udav

grass snake	сары жылан	sarı dʒılan
rattle snake	шакылдак жылан	ʃakıldak dʒılan
anaconda	анаконда	anakonda

lizard	кескелдирик	keskeldirik
iguana	игуана	iguana
monitor lizard	эчкемер	etʃkemer
salamander	саламандра	salamandra
chameleon	хамелеон	χameleon
scorpion	чаян	tʃajan

turtle	ташбака	taʃbaka
frog	бака	baka
toad	курбака	kurbaka
crocodile	крокодил	krokodil

93. Insects

insect, bug	курт-кумурска	kurt-kumurska
butterfly	көпөлөк	køpøløk
ant	кумурска	kumurska
fly	чымын	tʃımın
mosquito	чиркей	tʃirkej
beetle	коңуз	koŋuz

wasp	аары	aarı
bee	бал аары	bal aarı
bumblebee	жапан аары	dʒapan aarı
gadfly (botfly)	көгөөн	køgøøn

spider	жөргөмүш	dʒørgømyʃ
spiderweb	желе	dʒele

dragonfly	ийнелик	ijnelik
grasshopper	чегиртке	tʃegirtke
moth (night butterfly)	көпөлөк	køpøløk
cockroach	таракан	tarakan
tick	кене	kene
flea	бүргө	byrgø
midge	майда чымын	majda tʃımın
locust	чегиртке	tʃegirtke
snail	үлүл	ylyl
cricket	кара чегиртке	kara tʃegirtke
lightning bug	жалтырак коңуз	dʒaltırak koŋuz
ladybug	айланкөчөк	ajlankøtʃøk
cockchafer	саратан коңуз	saratan koŋuz
leech	сүлүк	sylyk
caterpillar	каз таман	kaz taman
earthworm	жер курту	dʒer kurtu
larva	курт	kurt

FLORA

94. Trees

tree	дарак	darak
deciduous (adj)	жалбырактуу	dʒalbıraktuu
coniferous (adj)	ийне жалбырактуулар	ijne dʒalbıraktuular
evergreen (adj)	дайым жашыл	dajım dʒaʃıl

apple tree	алма бак	alma bak
pear tree	алмурут бак	almurut bak
sweet cherry tree	гилас	gilas
sour cherry tree	алча	altʃa
plum tree	кара өрүк	kara øryk

birch	ак кайың	ak kajıŋ
oak	эмен	emen
linden tree	жөкө дарак	dʒøkø darak
aspen	бай терек	baj terek
maple	клён	klʲon

spruce	кара карагай	kara karagaj
pine	карагай	karagaj
larch	лиственница	listvennitsa
fir tree	пихта	piχta
cedar	кедр	kedr

poplar	терек	terek
rowan	четин	tʃetin
willow	мажүрүм тал	madʒyrym tal
alder	ольха	olʲχa

beech	бук	buk
elm	кара жыгач	kara dʒıgatʃ

ash (tree)	ясень	jasenʲ
chestnut	каштан	kaʃtan

magnolia	магнолия	magnolija
palm tree	пальма	palʲma
cypress	кипарис	kiparis

mangrove	мангро дарагы	mangro daragı
baobab	баобаб	baobab
eucalyptus	эвкалипт	evkalipt
sequoia	секвойя	sekvoja

95. Shrubs

bush	бадал	badal
shrub	бадал	badal
grapevine	жүзүм	dʒyzym
vineyard	жүзүмдүк	dʒyzymdyk
raspberry bush	дан куурай	dan kuuraj
blackcurrant bush	кара карагат	kara karagat
redcurrant bush	кызыл карагат	kızıl karagat
gooseberry bush	крыжовник	krıdʒovnik
acacia	акация	akatsija
barberry	бөрү карагат	børy karagat
jasmine	жасмин	dʒasmin
juniper	кара арча	kara artʃa
rosebush	роза бадалы	roza badalı
dog rose	ит мурун	it murun

96. Fruits. Berries

fruit	мөмө-жемиш	mømø-dʒemiʃ
fruits	мөмө-жемиш	mømø-dʒemiʃ
apple	алма	alma
pear	алмурут	almurut
plum	кара өрүк	kara øryk
strawberry (garden ~)	кулпунай	kulpunaj
sour cherry	алча	altʃa
sweet cherry	гилас	gilas
grape	жүзүм	dʒyzym
raspberry	дан куурай	dan kuuraj
blackcurrant	кара карагат	kara karagat
redcurrant	кызыл карагат	kızıl karagat
gooseberry	крыжовник	krıdʒovnik
cranberry	клюква	klukva
orange	апельсин	apelʲsin
mandarin	мандарин	mandarin
pineapple	ананас	ananas
banana	банан	banan
date	курма	kurma
lemon	лимон	limon
apricot	өрүк	øryk

peach	шабдаалы	ʃabdaalı
kiwi	киви	kivi
grapefruit	грейпфрут	grejpfrut

berry	жер жемиш	dʒer dʒemiʃ
berries	жер жемиштер	dʒer dʒemiʃter
cowberry	брусника	brusnika
wild strawberry	кызылгат	kızılgat
bilberry	кара моюл	kara mojʉl

97. Flowers. Plants

| flower | гүл | gyl |
| bouquet (of flowers) | десте | deste |

rose (flower)	роза	roza
tulip	жоогазын	dʒoogazın
carnation	гвоздика	gvozdika
gladiolus	гладиолус	gladiolus

cornflower	ботокөз	botokøz
harebell	коңгуроо гүл	koŋguroo gyl
dandelion	каакым-кукум	kaakım-kukum
camomile	ромашка	romaʃka

aloe	алоэ	aloe
cactus	кактус	kaktus
rubber plant, ficus	фикус	fikus

lily	лилия	lilija
geranium	герань	geranʲ
hyacinth	гиацинт	giatsint

mimosa	мимоза	mimoza
narcissus	нарцисс	nartsiss
nasturtium	настурция	nasturtsija

orchid	орхидея	orχideja
peony	пион	pion
violet	бинапша	binapʃa

pansy	алагүл	alagyl
forget-me-not	незабудка	nezabudka
daisy	маргаритка	margaritka

poppy	кызгалдак	kızgaldak
hemp	наша	naʃa
mint	жалбыз	dʒalbız
lily of the valley	ландыш	landıʃ
snowdrop	байчечекей	bajtʃetʃekej

nettle	чалкан	tʃalkan
sorrel	ат кулак	at kulak
water lily	чөмүч баш	tʃømytʃ baʃ
fern	папоротник	paporotnik
lichen	лишайник	liʃajnik

conservatory (greenhouse)	күнөскана	kynøskana
lawn	газон	gazon
flowerbed	клумба	klumba

plant	өсүмдүк	øsymdyk
grass	чөп	tʃøp
blade of grass	бир тал чөп	bir tal tʃøp

leaf	жалбырак	dʒalbɪrak
petal	гүлдүн желекчеси	gyldyn dʒelektʃesi
stem	сабак	sabak
tuber	жемиш тамыр	dʒemiʃ tamɪr

| young plant (shoot) | өсмө | øsmø |
| thorn | тикен | tiken |

to blossom (vi)	гүлдөө	gyldøø
to fade, to wither	соолуу	sooluu
smell (odor)	жыт	dʒɪt
to cut (flowers)	кесүү	kesyy
to pick (a flower)	үзүү	yzyy

98. Cereals, grains

grain	дан	dan
cereal crops	дан эгиндери	dan eginderi
ear (of barley, etc.)	машак	maʃak

wheat	буудай	buudaj
rye	кара буудай	kara buudaj
oats	сулу	sulu

| millet | таруу | taruu |
| barley | арпа | arpa |

corn	жүгөрү	dʒygøry
rice	күрүч	kyrytʃ
buckwheat	гречиха	gretʃiχa

pea plant	нокот	nokot
kidney bean	төө буурчак	tøø buurtʃak
soy	соя	soja
lentil	жасмык	dʒasmɪk
beans (pulse crops)	буурчак	buurtʃak

COUNTRIES OF THE WORLD

99. Countries. Part 1

Afghanistan	Ооганстан	ooganstan
Albania	Албания	albanija
Argentina	Аргентина	argentina
Armenia	Армения	armenija
Australia	Австралия	avstralija
Austria	Австрия	avstrija
Azerbaijan	Азербайжан	azerbajdʒan
The Bahamas	Багам аралдары	bagam araldarı
Bangladesh	Бангладеш	bangladeʃ
Belarus	Беларусь	belarusʲ
Belgium	Бельгия	belʲgija
Bolivia	Боливия	bolivija
Bosnia and Herzegovina	Босния жана	bosnija dʒana
Brazil	Бразилия	brazilija
Bulgaria	Болгария	bolgarija
Cambodia	Камбожа	kambodʒa
Canada	Канада	kanada
Chile	Чили	tʃili
China	Кытай	kıtaj
Colombia	Колумбия	kolumbija
Croatia	Хорватия	χorvatija
Cuba	Куба	kuba
Cyprus	Кипр	kipr
Czech Republic	Чехия	tʃeχija
Denmark	Дания	danija
Dominican Republic	Доминикан Республикасы	dominikan respublikası
Ecuador	Эквадор	ekvador
Egypt	Египет	egipet
England	Англия	anglija
Estonia	Эстония	estonija
Finland	Финляндия	finlʲandija
France	Франция	frantsija
French Polynesia	Француз Полинезиясы	frantsuz polinezijası
Georgia	Грузия	gruzija
Germany	Германия	germanija
Ghana	Гана	gana
Great Britain	Улуу Британия	uluu britanija

Greece	**Греция**	gretsija
Haiti	**Гаити**	gaiti
Hungary	**Венгрия**	vengrija

100. Countries. Part 2

Iceland	**Исландия**	islandija
India	**Индия**	indija
Indonesia	**Индонезия**	indonezija
Iran	**Иран**	iran
Iraq	**Ирак**	irak
Ireland	**Ирландия**	irlandija
Israel	**Израиль**	izrailʲ
Italy	**Италия**	italija
Jamaica	**Ямайка**	jamajka
Japan	**Япония**	japonija
Jordan	**Иордания**	iordanija
Kazakhstan	**Казакстан**	kazakstan
Kenya	**Кения**	kenija
Kirghizia	**Кыргызстан**	kırgızstan
Kuwait	**Кувейт**	kuvejt
Laos	**Лаос**	laos
Latvia	**Латвия**	latvija
Lebanon	**Ливан**	livan
Libya	**Ливия**	livija
Liechtenstein	**Лихтенштейн**	liχtenʃtejn
Lithuania	**Литва**	litva
Luxembourg	**Люксембург**	lʉksemburg
Macedonia (Republic of ~)	**Македония**	makedonija
Madagascar	**Мадагаскар**	madagaskar
Malaysia	**Малазия**	malazija
Malta	**Мальта**	malʲta
Mexico	**Мексика**	meksika
Moldova, Moldavia	**Молдова**	moldova
Monaco	**Монако**	monako
Mongolia	**Монголия**	mongolija
Montenegro	**Черногория**	tʃernogorija
Morocco	**Марокко**	marokko
Myanmar	**Мьянма**	mjanma
Namibia	**Намибия**	namibija
Nepal	**Непал**	nepal
Netherlands	**Нидерланддар**	niderlanddar
New Zealand	**Жаңы Зеландия**	dʒaŋɨ zelandija
North Korea	**Түндүк Корея**	tundyk koreja
Norway	**Норвегия**	norvegija

101. Countries. Part 3

Pakistan	Пакистан	pakistan
Palestine	Палестина	palestina
Panama	Панама	panama
Paraguay	Парагвай	paragvaj
Peru	Перу	peru
Poland	Польша	polʲʃa
Portugal	Португалия	portugalija
Romania	Румыния	rumınija
Russia	Россия	rossija
Saudi Arabia	Сауд Аравиясы	saud aravijası
Scotland	Шотландия	ʃotlandija
Senegal	Сенегал	senegal
Serbia	Сербия	serbija
Slovakia	Словакия	slovakija
Slovenia	Словения	slovenija
South Africa	ТАР	tar
South Korea	Түштүк Корея	tyʃtyk koreja
Spain	Испания	ispanija
Suriname	Суринам	surinam
Sweden	Швеция	ʃvetsija
Switzerland	Швейцария	ʃvejtsarija
Syria	Сирия	sirija
Taiwan	Тайвань	tajvanʲ
Tajikistan	Тажикистан	tadʒikistan
Tanzania	Танзания	tanzanija
Tasmania	Тасмания	tasmanija
Thailand	Таиланд	tailand
Tunisia	Тунис	tunis
Turkey	Түркия	tyrkija
Turkmenistan	Туркмения	turkmenija
Ukraine	Украина	ukraina
United Arab Emirates	Бириккен Араб Эмираттары	birikken arab emirattarı
United States of America	Америка Кошмо Штаттары	amerika koʃmo ʃtattarı
Uruguay	Уругвай	urugvaj
Uzbekistan	Өзбекистан	øzbekistan
Vatican	Ватикан	vatikan
Venezuela	Венесуэла	venesuela
Vietnam	Вьетнам	vjetnam
Zanzibar	Занзибар	zanzibar